THE
ELECTRONIC
BATTLEFIELD

THE
ELECTRONIC
BATTLEFIELD

Paul Dickson

INDIANA UNIVERSITY PRESS
Bloomington & London

Published in Canada by Fitzhenry & Whiteside Limited, Don Mills, Ontario

Manufactured in the United States of America

Library of Congress Cataloging in Publication Data
Dickson, Paul.
The electronic battlefield.

Bibliography
Includes index.
1. Electronics in military engineering.
2. Military art and science—Automation.   I. Title.
UG485.D5   1976   355.4   75-31342
ISBN 0-253-12158-2   1 2 3 4 5 80 79 78 77 76

For my son Andrew

CONTENTS

Photographs on pages 55–70 and 143–158

ACKNOWLEDGMENTS

I thank my good friend Bob Skole for insisting that I should do this project in the first place and thank Nancy Dickson for all her help in its preparation. I would also like to thank the Fund for Investigative Journalism for a small grant that enabled me to purchase reams of reports on various elements of the electronic battlefield to sift for nuggets. For their part in helping me track down information I would like to acknowledge the particular aid of the members of the MITRE Corporation's Department of Sensor Systems Applications and the staff of NARMIC, National Action Research on the Military Industrial Complex.

THE
ELECTRONIC
BATTLEFIELD

ONE

Glimpses

War is no longer the desperate annihilating struggle that it was
. . . . It is a warfare of limited aims. This is not to say that
. . . the conduct of war has become less bloodthirsty or more
chivalrous. On the contrary. . . . But in a physical sense war
involves very small numbers of people, mostly highly trained
specialists. The fighting . . . takes place on the vague frontiers
whose whereabouts the average man can only guess at . . . .
—*George Orwell*, 1984.

*To avoid any possible confusion, the material in this introductory
chapter to an otherwise nonfiction book is fictional. However, while
the people and events in the following section are completely fictional,
the rest of the book will show that the hardware, the systems, and the
type of war depicted are not.*

NORTH STAR

Major Reed Higgins, USAF, woke to the chirp of his special
Pageboy IV communications set lying a few feet from his bed.
With only a little fumbling he hit the illuminated receiver button
and the number three began pulsing on the set's tiny video display
screen.

Despite the fact that he was still half asleep he had no trouble recalling the word-for-word meaning of the three that had been drilled into him so many times.

YOU HAVE ONE HOUR IN WHICH TO BE AT YOUR ASSIGNED STATION AND READY FOR COMBAT OPERATIONS. IF YOU NEED TRANSPORTATION TO YOUR STATION: SIGNAL 4. IF YOU HAVE ANY OTHER PROBLEM THAT PREVENTS YOU FROM GETTING TO YOUR STATION: SIGNAL 6. IF YOU ARE READY AND WILL BE ON STATION WITHIN THE ALLOTED HOUR: SIGNAL 8.

As his suburban Arlington townhouse was only ten minutes down Interstate-66 from the new Westmoreland Annex to the Pentagon near Springfield he tapped the eight on the Pageboy without even thinking. Now more awake he carefully noted that the time was seven minutes past midnight, which meant that he had gotten close to four hours' sleep. He had been warned the day before that there would probably be some action tonight, so he had left work early, played nine holes of golf, eaten a light, early dinner, and was in bed a few minutes after eight.

After he dressed—he opted for a sports shirt and slacks over his uniform because of the hour and the heat—he woke his wife to the point where she was able to understand that he was on his way to "night ops," and she noted before drifting back to sleep that he would be home in the morning and that, perhaps, after he had gotten some more sleep, the family could swim in the afternoon. It was a most pleasing thought because the Washington area was locked into one of its famous hot and humid periods.

Stopping only for a quick cup of black coffee and a piece of toast he was soon in his car and on his way to the Annex. After the quick drive in his air-conditioned Subaru-Dodge he slipped into one of the red-lined night ops parking spaces under the Annex and headed down in an elevator to the third sub-basement and the bombproof, remote, combat center. He opened the outer door with a press of his right thumb against a special plate, which checked his thumbprint against its digitized facsimile in one of the center's computers, and headed for the manned checkpoint where he asked the Corporal on duty, "What've we got tonight?"

"They don't tell me much, Major," he replied. "But it's a live one in the NATO area. The first shift has been in there for almost four hours now. Good luck."

Higgins took a short-cut through the heavily air-conditioned computer room and along a short corridor into the briefing room where he stopped at the door for a second cup of coffee at the hot drink machine. He then walked over to a large electronic status board that informed him that he was to sit at briefing terminal 14. As he sat in the large, plush, swivel chair in front of the console he looked at the digital clock built in above it and noticed that it was now 0037. After a few moments drinking the hot coffee, Higgins pushed the button marked READY TO BE BRIEFED and went through a quick series of identifying procedures which proved to the apparatus in front of him that he was indeed Major Reed Higgins. The following message then came on the screen in soothing green letters:

BACKGROUND.
SECRET: US & NATO ONLY.
Abbreviated Situation Report #14. Updated through 0030 hours.

US technical aid has been extended to a European Freeland Ally against Hostilian insurgents in that nation who have conducted sapper raids against a number of sites within the country including several important factories, isolated Freeland military and civil police bases and a USAF radar installation. The US has agreed not to put men in on the ground and any required manned operations will be conducted by Freeland military. The US, NATO II, and Freeland all are agreed that the operation should be completed in the quickest possible time to avert further insurgent mobilization and adverse public reaction in Freeland as well as other countries. After several days of covert reconnaissance by unattended ground sensors and airborne satellite and remotely piloted aircraft sensing devices, a number of Hostilian targets were located and programmed into the attack plan. After final Presidential approval, operations against the Hostilians commenced at 2041 hours last night. The code name for the operation is NORTH STAR. Action against the Hostilians has been heavy and fruitful during the early hours of the engagement with sensor-triggered ordnance, antipersonnel cruise missiles, laser-guided smart bombs and Kamikaze-type remotely piloted vehicle raids yielding a heavy toll of men and equipment. Our midnight satellite report indicates that more than half (56.6%) of the targets programmed for this operation have either been destroyed or severely crippled and that the operation can be expected to be completed by 0500 hours. Do you have any questions concerning the general situation?

Higgins, 40, who had converted from being a pilot in a manned aircraft to a pilot in charge of a remotely piloted vehicle (or RPV) three years earlier, still had trouble with some of the customs and procedures associated with this new kind of flying—not the least of which was being briefed by a machine. One question he wanted to ask and, indeed, felt he would always want to ask in these situations, was what country is Freeland and who are her Hostilians? These terms, which had first been used in stateside exercises during the long war in Southeast Asia to represent respectively the old Republic of South Vietnam and the Viet Cong/North Vietnamese, had over time become Pentagonese for any allied nation and her guerrilla insurgents. He strongly suspected that in situations like pilot's briefings the terms were used to keep those being briefed from getting rattled by too direct a realization that there were real people about to be involved on the other end of a remote strike. The computer would not give up the real names if asked—although few ever tried—so he decided to give the console the OK to continue the briefing. Ironically, he had a pretty good idea of where the action was taking place anyway from what he had read in the papers and he'd find out for sure later in the morning when it was all summarized once the action was over.

The briefing continued:

> Major Higgins, your duty will be to pilot two laser designator RPVs that will be used to illuminate Hostilian targets for smart bomb delivery. The two aircraft, LRPV-456 and LRPV-457, are now airborne and under the control of another pilot, Capt. John E. Elliott, who you will be replacing at 0120 hours. The events you will take part in are numbers 331 through 339. When you signal that you are ready, descriptions of these events will be put on the screen so that you can familiarize yourself with them. They do not have to be memorized because they will be on the screen in your cockpit in the combat center along with the proper NORTH STAR maps.

"Bird dog work," he thought, "not exciting like remote dogfighting, but not as unnerving as Kamikaze missions with expendable RPVs."

He had first flown in combat in Vietnam in 1970, back when RPVs were experimental items that pilots didn't quite take seriously. On three occasions over the next two years he had brought back badly damaged planes to his base in Thailand and he prided himself on his ability to keep his plane in the air. For this reason piloting Kamikaze RPVs, which were not supposed to return, ran against the grain. But the younger pilots who had only flown RPVs—the ones the older ones called the "pinball wizards" because of their amusement park-like attitude towards combat— seemed to love the Kamikaze missions. Tonight's work simply called for following predesignated routes to target areas, locating the assigned target by means of the package of sensing devices aboard the plane (including a small high-resolution infrared camera that permitted him to see on the ground much better than he could have with his eyes from a real plane), locking onto the target with a laser beam from the plane and waiting for a smart bomb dropped many miles away that would be guided in to the target along the laser beam. He asked for his events, which showed up on the screen looking like this:

EVENT LIST FOR MAJOR REED HIGGINS, USAF.
ALL TIMES LOCAL TO WASHINGTON.

EVENT	TIME	UNIT	ASSIGNMENT
331	0125	LRPV-456	Proceed to NORTH STAR grid number 304 along Route AA. Route roughly follows small river, which will be marked on your map as Cowhouse Creek. Proceed to the Northwest quadrant of grid 304, reduce altitude, and begin systematic search, using all available sensor data, for a carefully-hidden Hostilian base camp known to exist in this mountainous area. Laser-designate when found.
EVENT	TIME	UNIT	ASSIGNMENT
332	0135	LRPV-457	Proceed to NORTH STAR grid number 298 along Route BL. We are attempting to locate an antiaircraft emplacement along this Route and would like to draw fire from it in order to locate it. Therefore, you are to fly low to present the Hostilian battery with an attractive target. Immediately report any hostile fire. Upon arrival in 298 take your plane to cruising altitude and begin a systematic reconnaissance sweep of the entire grid looking for Hostilian food and weapons caches we strongly suspect to be in the area. Depending on your needs, smart bombs or cruise

missiles will be provided in less than
five minutes for targets in this grid.

Scanning the rest of the list, Higgins saw that the other events
were pretty much like the routine 331 and that 332 was going to be
the most interesting and challenging. What he particularly liked
was the opportunity it provided for him to do some evasive flying
as he attracted enemy fire. He studied the list for a few minutes
and shut off the briefing console. With about 20 minutes still to go
before he took over his pair of planes from Captain Elliott, he
decided to kill 15 of them reading a magazine in the pilot's lounge
after which he wandered into the combat center to peer over the
other pilot's shoulder to see how his planes were behaving. To his
dismay, he found that Elliott was ahead of schedule and already
in the process of flying 457 low as part of event 332. Normally one
pilot would not think of moving in on another's events, but it was
different tonight because the order was out to move as quickly as
possible and get the whole thing over in less than ten hours. Then
less than two minutes before he was to take over the screen, which
showed the picture from the front of 457, it began to jiggle
radically for a second and then return to normal. On the third
jiggle the picture went blank. The plane had been fired upon and
all that Elliott had done was keep it flying straight ahead and push
the position marking device so that the spot would be located for
attack. Higgins was angry with Elliott for not trying to save the
plane but would say nothing right now.

Immediately after the hit the electronic event board registered
a change. The rest of event 332 was being reassigned to another
plane and pilot and all that remained for Higgins to do was to
laser-designate Hostilians and their camps.

"Damn!" he thought. "It's going to be a dull night."

THE MORNING AFTER

Frank and Barbara Hall slept through the first alarm from
their clock radio, but woke on the second series of buzzes at 7:50,

which meant that the time before they both left for work would be a bit more hectic than if they had responded to the 7:40 alarm. Frank did his normal ten minutes of wake-up exercises in eight in order to get to the kitchen TV in time to turn on the eight o'clock NBC News, which was part of the Hall morning routine. As the last moments of the Today Show's first hour interview played out—something about a redoubled Federal effort to support the arts—the Halls began scurrying in earnest: dressing, preparing breakfast and taking turns in the bathroom. By the time the news actually began, Frank was brushing and water-picking his teeth and Barbara was in the bedroom closet looking for the shoes she wanted to drop off to be repaired during her lunch hour.

The news began:

Good Morning. Today is June 15, 1985.

Earlier this morning the White House and the Office of the Joint Chiefs of Staff announced the successful completion of an unmanned tri-service military action during the night. Details are sparse at this point but the action took place between approximately 8:45 last night and 4:45 this morning.

The action centered on bands of radical Basque separatists operating in the northern Spanish provinces of Vizcaya and Guizpucoa. These guerrillas have been a major source of irritation to the Spanish government—the former Franco regime and the current monarchy—for more than 15 years. In the last year, however, the insurgents have gained substantial new strength and, with that strength, boldness. In late May, the Basques initiated a coordinated series of raids against government and industrial sites in northern Spain, which left more than 100 Spanish regular military and civil police dead, and millions of dollars of property damage in their wake.

According to the White House the US offered electronic aid at the request of Spain and the realigned North American Treaty Organization (NATO II), which includes Spain. Intelligence reports indicated that the Basques were readying another guerrilla offensive and it was additionally feared that a new offensive might have the effect of giving encouragement to a growing Catalan Independence Movement in the area around Barcelona to the east of the Basque area. The White House added that the final decision was made to render electronic aid early yesterday after which the President took the time to advise key Congressional leaders. Because American troops were not directly involved and because the engagement was to take less than 48 hours there was—under the provisions of the new War Powers Act—no need to call the whole Congress or any of its committees into formal session.

The number of targets located and hit numbered over 250, which, again according to the White House, is believed to have been more than enough to break the back of the movement. The number of Basque dead and wounded has not been officially estimated—and will not be until after Spanish troops complete their post-electronic sweep of the area—but an Associated Press report quotes an unnamed Pentagon source as having said that he wouldn't be at all surprised if the total was in excess of 1,500 casualties.

The actual collection of equipment used in this particular strike against the guerrillas in Spain is called the Counter-Insurgency Package or COINPAC. We will now move to our science and technology editor who is in Washington to explain this latest electronic strike:

This is Tom Bishop in Washington.

Unlike last spring's Bolivian strike or the quick succession of Middle Eastern strikes last November—all of which were mounted against standing armies—last night's strike or mini-war used a special package of techniques and equipment called COINPAC, which is specifically tailored for use against irregulars in guerrilla operations. One is hard pressed to know where to begin in describing the many individual types of equipment which are part of COINPAC but. . . .

As a quick summary of each of the key COINPAC systems was given, the Halls continued to go about their morning business paying only scant attention to the television. When they both finally sat down for breakfast and were prepared to pay full attention to what was going on, the science editor was just finishing.

Incidently, there is an interesting footnote to last night's activities. Important pieces of the action were watched on TV at the White House *live* thanks to special high-resolution cameras aboard the new SURVSATCOM satellite. While this system has been used before, this is the first time, we are told, that the key events from the beginning to the end of the conflict were televised. A White House spokesman has indicated that a special "sanitized" and condensed version of the strike will be released for public viewing. This is Tom Bishop in Washington. Now back to New York.

Thank you, Tom, I should point out that we have gotten later word indicating that those tapes will be released in time for rebroadcast on the evening news tonight.

Meanwhile, there has been little response from Congress although it is expected that several dissident Senators and Representatives opposed to the increasing use of the electronic strike will hold a press conference later this morning.

As the newscaster moved to the other events of the day, Frank asked his wife, "Did you catch any of that?"

"Not much," she replied. "Something about a war. Spain or Portugal I think. Whatever it was, it's over."

"Good. So there's nothing to worry about."

McNamara's Band

"You have made continued progress. Cain did his murder
with a club; the Hebrews did their murders with javelins and
swords; the Greeks and Romans added protective armor and
the fine art of military organization and generalship; the
Christian has added guns and gunpowder; a few centuries
from now he will have so greatly improved the deadly
effectiveness of his weapons of slaughter that all men will
confess that without Christian civilization war must have
remained a poor and trifling thing to the end of time."
                              —*Words from Satan in Mark Twain's*
                              The Mysterious Stranger.

IN A FROG'S EYE

During the Second World War the Nazis fielded a weapon on
a limited basis that the Americans immediately dubbed the
"doodlebug." Except that it carried high explosives set to explode
on contact, it was a comical affair about the size of a baby
carriage that chugged about jerkily under the control of a soldier
who directed it remotely by means of a control box to which it
was attached by wires. The object was to get the doodlebug to
crash into a target and presumably explode before it was stopped
by small arms fire, fell into a trench, or got its wires cut.

With its limited range and the ease with which it could be

foiled, among other shortcomings, it was hardly a weapon that kept Allied leaders from sleeping at night. But it did serve to underscore in its own awkward manner a point about fighting that was first made when man moved from hitting other men with his hand to throwing rocks. The point: success at war means inflicting the greatest damage from the furthest distance.

Doodlebugs notwithstanding, each time a true advance in the destructive power or distance of a weapon takes place, the character of war changes. When man was less militarily sophisticated centuries separated such turning points. That is why, for instance, the Battle of Agincourt of 1415 stands out so clearly as a beacon. War was forever changed at that encounter as the French were defeated by a much smaller British army because their weapons for close-in man-to-man combat were no match for the English longbows.

The process of change continued picking up speed right into modern times when, with the advent of atomic weapons and intercontinental ballistic missiles, it became clear that there are certain limits to change. These weapons have effectively taken the concept of all-out war to its logical conclusion. After all, larger bombs, missiles with multiple nuclear warheads, and missiles that can be fired from under the sea are really just refinements and variations on the theme that millions can be killed halfway around the world at the push of a button.

Soon after the atomic missile change came the realization that unless we wanted to destroy vast chunks, if not all, of the world, a step back from the nuclear brink had to be taken, which meant continued reliance on conventional, non-nuclear means of fighting for the foreseeable future. In the early 1960s, in the wake of this realization, another change began to take place that will have the precise kind of effect just detailed in scenario form.

This change itself was born of the technological feast that was served up in America in the decade after Sputnik, thanks in large measure to the massive support of research and development by the federal government, which totalled about $100 billion for the decade—an astounding total even in light of the inflated dollars of the post–Nixon era. These huge amounts of money made it possible for new ideas, devices, techniques, and refinements to be presented with awesome regularity. For the science and technology subculture it was a period of unprecedented bonanza when there were more new ideas—and funds with which to pursue them—than there were applications for those ideas. For instance, in 1960 an intriguing item called the laser was invented, which by releasing energy stored in the structure of certain materials is able to produce a beam of light so concentrated that it does not dissipate over distance. Long called "the device in search of itself," it is only now, more than fifteen years later, that a fairly long list of uses has been compiled for the laser.

Three developments occurred in the 1960s that can be identified as the technological base for the change that this book contends will do for conventional warfare what the atomic missile revolution did for total war; that is, to bring it to its logical end point—in this case not only distance from the enemy but destructive precision.

The first development was the so-called electronics revolution, a verbal catch-all for a situation in which an established industry growing at a relatively fast rate came into the 1960s and surpassed the most optimistic predictions of industry boosters. This was not only a matter of dollar volume (which went from a billion dollars a year in 1950 to $25 billion by 1970) but could be measured too in terms of the rate and level of innovation and the ability of electronic devices themselves. For instance, a technique called LSI (for Large Scale Integration) was introduced in which hundreds of thousands of already "miniaturized" transistors, resistors, and the like could be crammed onto a very small surface allowing for, say, the placement of the equivalent of a thousand radio tubes on a surface no bigger than a shirt button. This permitted many things including the development of electronic devices of great complexity small enough to be tucked into a soldier's backpack or under the instrument panel of a jet fighter. At the same time, the number of copies of electronics' most famous and versatile end product, the digital computer, grew at an astonishing rate. Back in the early 1950s when the ground-breaking Univac I was delivered to the United States Bureau of the Census, experts in this new field predicted a market for units of all types that might reach several dozen in the near future, but certainly not many more than 100 could be sold by 1970. As it turned out, the American computer population in 1970 was reaching 200,000 machines. Taken together, the implications of just these two developments, let alone others, boil down to the fact that the nation was getting vastly increased computing power and much greater electronic mobility.

Beyond electronics, the second new development of the 1960s was the appearance of still early, yet sophisticated, remotely manned systems (often heavily dependent on electronics as a matter of fact) that clearly demonstrated that machines under man's control were quite capable of doing his dirty work. There were many good examples from the period with dozens coming from the unmanned portion of the space program alone, but two of the most dramatic and commonly cited are the cases of CURV and Surveyor 3.* On April 7, 1966, an unmanned sub called CURV (Cable Controlled Underwater Research Vehicle), equipped with a TV camera and a simple grappling device, went in and picked up the H-bomb that the United States had lost in the Mediterranean off the coast of Spain. Most significantly, this came after attempts by more cumbersome manned subs had failed. The following year the unmanned Lunar Surveyor 3 craft landed on the moon, where, under the control of operators at the Jet

---

* Their popularity as examples doubtlessly stems from their use in an influential paper, "Remotely Manned Systems—Origins and Current Capabilities," by Terrell E. Greene of the RAND Corporation.

Propulsion Laboratory in California, a clawlike device was to dig a small trench and place the soil from it into a special apparatus where it would be analyzed. This time, however, the soil-analysis package became stuck in its container and the mission was in jeopardy. However, those on the ground decided to guide the hand over to the package where it would give it a tap in the hope that that would dislodge it which it did. Employing machines as man's extended self was nothing new as a concept, but the 1960s brought that concept to true, sophisticated reality, or, at least far enough along to allow him to put his hand on the moon—a feat that for the public was lost in the excitement of the manned moon landing, but that was duly noted by the technical community.

The third new development was the emergence of bionics and to a lesser extent other new models and clues for innovation. Bionics is the curious marriage of biology and engineering in which living systems, rather than mechanics, math, or physics as such, provide the keys to new invention. Plagiarizing nature, of course, predated the 1960s in such cases as sonar with its direct parallels to the bat's sounding system, swim flippers for humans copied from web-footed aquatic life, and computer pioneers who were aware that part of their model was the human brain; but it was not until the 1960s that this concept moved from occasional and informal borrowing from natural design to a concerted effort to exploit the natural world. Sponsored in large measure by the military—which also named the new science through Major Jack Steele of the Air Force's Air Development Division—its generally acknowledged moment of birth was the First Air Force Bionics Symposium, which began on September 13, 1960.*

---

* Many laymen have only heard the term bionics used in the context of the TV show *The Six-Million Dollar Man* on which the hero, who was badly maimed in an accident, was rebuilt at a cost of $6 million through bionics. While the ability to rebuild portrayed on the show is fanciful and far beyond the state of the art, the term is not misused since one arm, so to speak, of bionics is at work developing better artificial human parts.

Initially, at least, the science of bionics was the science of knowing where and why to look. It was soon axiomatic that the ideal for information storage was not the library or the computer but the human gene; that the best navigation systems for air and sea were not human inventions but were contained in the bodies of birds and sea mammals; and that the ideal communications network was not AT&T but the human body. Not only could life systems themselves be useful but so could their life history. Humans could learn and possibly copy from the success of an animal that had been on the earth for 2,000,000 years, and be studied for copying while extinct animals could be studied for potential "errors."

Significantly, the speakers at the 1960 symposium made it abundantly clear that there was military value in all of this, and one specified that the Air Force was specifically interested in three aspects of living prototypes: the sensors (or sensory receptors) of animals, the integrating action of their nervous systems, and their ability to store and retrieve information. This was hardly idle talk and it soon became evident that the military—or, more precisely, scientists and engineers working for the military—had become truly fascinated by certain animal systems, especially in the sensory field. Papers with titles like "Sensing Partial Failure—A Step Toward Self-Healing" and "Human Processing of Olfactory Information" began to appear with regularity. Despite their dry, stiff titles, the papers were asking and hinting at answers to fascinating questions: Can a manmade electronic system be configured to sense a malfunction in the same way that a human feels pain? And once located, can a process be built that duplicates human healing of, say, a broken arm? Or, would it be possible to copy the highly sensitive animal sense of smell in a remote device that could literally smell an enemy and transmit that information back to a central point comparable to the brain?

Of all the bionic images and questions of the time, however, few were quite as tantalizing to the military as those having to do with the eye of a frog. Early research revealed some one million receptors in a frog's eye of which there were five types, each with a separate function. One type is a bug detector that exclusively tells the frog that food is on the way and to which the frog automatically reacts by devouring it. Another set of detectors only registers the slightest dimming of light, which causes the frog to automatically jump into water, which is picked up by another class of sensors. A slight dimming of light is exactly what happens when the shadow of a bird passes, which makes this a prime defense system. As each class of sensors does not bother with anything other than what it is looking for, and since each class is able to spot and respond simultaneously to stimuli without even having to go to the brain for processing, this looked like the perfect sensor system with the very abilities that radar and computer engineers dreamed about. Shortly a number of researchers were looking into frogs' eyes and RCA was actually at work on a rough $200,000 replica.

Meanwhile, it quickly became obvious that there was more to this than theory, model building, and research for the sake of research. Daniel S. Halacy was able to report when his book, *Bionics the Science of 'Living' Machines*, was published in 1965 a number of real applications including a working gyroscopic control unit patterned directly on the orientation and control system of the common housefly, a widely used technique for sharper television imagery based on the image intensification system at work in the eye of a horseshoe crab, and an airborne ground speed indicator built for the Air Force from plans abstracted from the flight system of a beetle.

These three developments—electronics in general, remotely manned systems, and bionics—made possible the "electronic battlefield," which actually came about from a tactical rather than a technical challenge.

WHAT JASON DID
FOR THE SUMMER

To draw a line which your opponent must not cross over and then to back it up with physical strength is an idea as old as war itself, and has been at play in human endeavors as diverse as the Great Wall of China, the Maginot Line of the First World War, and the common street fight. However, the very thought of fighting from a front seemed altogether out of place in Vietnam where America's opponent struck from the shadows and from all sides. The United States countered with its own nonlinear tactics and techniques like "airmobile blankets," operational area defenses (or 360-degree fronts), carpet bombing, omnidirectional search and destroy missions, and more.

Yet in early 1966, despite these new tactics with their highly efficient sounding names and the statistics-laden testimonials made for them in Pentagon press briefings, one thing became clear to the war's American managers: men and supplies from the North were moving into the South with alarming ease. American bombing of the North, which had begun in earnest a year earlier under the appropriate code name of Rolling Thunder, had neither slowed the infiltration of the South nor shown any sign of bringing the war to a close. Instead, Hanoi's position had hardened, there was no evidence that the bombing was rushing the Communists to the bargaining table, and infiltration of the South was actually intensifying rather than slowing with the Demilitarized Zone (DMZ) serving as the prime gateway South.

The thoughts of some moved back to the barrier, which just might work in a guerrilla warfare situation. In fact, in the late 1950s the French had set up a barrier to block Tunisian infiltration into Algeria. That combination of old (barbed wire, land mines) and new (radar, listening devices) barrier elements had met with success. The United States had halfheartedly studied the idea of a barrier across Vietnam a good half-dozen times since 1958 when it was first looked at by American "advisors." The idea had never been rejected outright but rather it kept getting shelved as a superfluous notion in light of the belief that heavy infiltration could always be stopped with heavy bombing. However, the idea was presented once again in January, 1966, this time by Roger Fisher of Harvard Law School in one of periodic memos on defense matters that he sent to his friend the Assistant Secretary of Defense John McNaughton. As it turned out the timing was perfect because McNaughton, McNamara, and others were beginning to shop around for a better idea to stem the infiltration. Fisher's timely memo pointed out that a barrier would cut the traffic at the Laotian panhandle and the DMZ. Physically, he envisioned a mix of barbed wire, mines and chemical weapons that would be seeded and reseeded from the air. It would be about 10 miles wide and 160 miles long and would be flanked on either side by a wide defoliated free-fire zone.

McNaughton dwelt on the Fisher memo for about six weeks and then—adding some revisions of his own—passed it along to McNamara, who, in turn, asked for field reaction to the idea, specifically that of Admiral U. S. Grant Sharp, then commander of the Pacific forces. Sharp was less than friendly to the idea and cited a long list of foreseeable problems including the belief that it would take up to four years to create, tie up seven or eight United States divisions, strain the supply system, and probably not work after all. This strong opposition notwithstanding, the barrier idea showed enough merit to McNamara and his staff to get them to put the Army to work in March on "interdiction devices" that might be used in the system.

Meanwhile, at about the same time the Army was beginning its work, four top scientists from MIT and Harvard asked McNamara if he would like to see a large group of highly regarded scientists spend the summer months looking into possible "technical" solutions to the Vietnam dilemma. As the situation was not improving and was causing considerable frustration in official Washington, it was with genuine relief and hope that McNamara accepted the suggestion.

When the summer study was suggested in 1966 the group that the scientists belonged to was little known even to other scientists. Called the Jason Division or simply the Jasons, the group was composed of about 45 of the nation's top university scientists including several Nobel laureates. Jason had been organized in 1959 by the Institute for Defense Analyses, the influential military think tank, to serve as a highly sophisticated by-invitation-only brainstorming team that would spend certain weekends and summers wrestling with questions of new military technology. Each summer the Jasons and their families packed up and headed for a remote spot, where under a heavy security guard they spent a few hours each day on the summer's assignment, whether it be ballistic missiles or tactical nuclear weapons. While Jason had spent its early summers looking at matters that were concerned with weapons technology in the general sense, it began turning its attention to Vietnam in 1964, and it was only natural that it should suggest an overall technical review of the war as its summer of 1966 project.

In formally responding to the suggestion, McNamara in a letter of April 16 asked the group to look into one idea in particular: ". . . a fence across the infiltration trails, warning systems, reconnaissance (especially night) methods, night vision devices, defoliation techniques and area denial weapons." (Area denial is Pentagonese for so devastating, mining, or otherwise disturbing an area that use of it is denied to the enemy.) Most significantly, the McNamara letter signalled a departure from Fisher's original idea, which only depended on mines, pits, barbed wire, and other physical deterrents, to one laden with state-of-the-art electronic devices.

While the exact moment that the move to electronics took place has defied pinpointing, the reason has not: independently, each of the three services had developed or was in the process of developing equipment for remote detection and surveillance. In fact, the Army had been working in this area as far back as 1953 when, as part of its top secret Project Tacit, which was launched to improve its combat intelligence gathering, it had prototype acoustic and seismic sensors designed and built by the Operations Research Office at Johns Hopkins University. These devices were shipped to Korea in 1954 and tested in the Chorwon Valley area a little more than a year after the armistice had been signed. Although they arrived too late for that war, they showed that they might come in handy in some future conflict, as they could pick up clues that not only allowed detection of vehicles but could actually distinguish a jeep from a tank. The final report on this test system (called TABODA for Target Acquisition by Omnidirectional Detectors) was that large quantities of these sensors could be produced in a fairly short time.

What McNamara and his advisors saw was a new technology in search of a big, prominent, and challenging assignment and the "fence" fit the bill perfectly. The summer got underway as the 47 Jasons (augmented by 20 analysts from the Institute for Defense Analyses) met in Wellesley, Massachusetts beginning on June 13 for ten days of briefings by representatives of the military, CIA, White House, and State Department staffs. The group then split into four teams that were each to spend July and most of August in isolation working on one aspect of the problem. The exact site of the Jason summer, incidently, was Dana Hall, an exclusive prep school for girls in Wellesley.

On August 30 the report was delivered to McNamara personally by a delegation of Jasons. It was immediately regarded as so sensitive and potentially crucial that the only people outside of McNamara and his immediate staff to see it were General Wheeler and presidential aide W. W. Rostow. For an opening salvo it strongly condemned the increased bombing of the North from a tactical standpoint, the actual first sentence of the report reading: "As of July, 1966, the US bombing of North Vietnam had had no measurable direct effect on Hanoi's ability to mount and support military operations in the South at the current level."

Essentially the worthlessness of the Rolling Thunder campaign was not because American bombs were not exploding or hitting their designated targets; but, as the report asserted in no uncertain terms, because of the nature of the nation being bombed and the way it was waging the war. Because the North was basically a nation of subsistence farmers with little industry that was obtaining most of its military hardware from the USSR and China, the bombs had little effect on the operation of the country, its waging of the war, or its ability to shuttle troops and equipment south. The actual damage done in a year's bombing was "moderate" and the costs were more than absorbed by Moscow and Peking. The Jasons had analyzed intelligence reports and had come to the conclusion that the bombing had only done about $86 million in damage to date while the aid that poured into Hanoi from its allies was on the order of $250 to $400 million. It was not unreasonable to assume that more intensive American bombing would increase the flow of military and economic aid from the USSR and China.

North Vietnam's relatively primitive nature appeared to be its best defense against America's awesome airpower. Even its transportation system, which had suffered considerable damage, had not been seriously impaired by American bombers. The nation's countermeasure to bombed roads and rail lines was a vast supply of laborers who were able to repair and rebuild continually. The motley collection of Chinese trucks, old trains, crude watercraft, bicycles, animal-drawn carts, and human porters added up to a whole that was very primitive, very flexible, and very hard to hurt in any permanent way because it was not concentrated. For example, in the matter of enemy petroleum American air power is well suited to destroying tankers on the seas, large refineries and long tanker-truck convoys, but not for sampans or human porters moving a few gallons south at night.*

The Jasons concluded that these factors had not only kept the bombs that had fallen from having an effect but that not even an *expanded* campaign in the future would keep Hanoi from moving men and supplies south at the current or at an *increased* rate. The scholars did not doubt that North Vietnam was capable of "substantially increasing" its support of operations in the South.

If that were not enough, those who had prepared the report were unable to come up with any evidence supporting the oft-heard assumption that the bombs were weakening the communists' will to fight. The assumption was discharged as one that was overlooking such basics as ". . . the fact, well-documented in the historical and social scientific literature, that a direct frontal attack on a society tends to strengthen the social fabric of the nation, to increase popular support of the existing government, to improve the determination of both the leadership and the populace to fight back, to induce a variety of protective measures that reduce the society's vulnerability to future attack, and to develop an increased capacity for quick repair and restoration of essential functions." That "iconoclastic" view of the effect of the bombs on morale echoed a statement in the original Fisher memo, which said, "There is some evidence that bombings have resulted in an increased DRV [Democratic Republic of Vietnam] resolve to continue the war to an eventual victory."

With the bombing completely condemned, an alternative solution was in order. The report spelled out in considerable detail the alternative it felt was most likely to succeed, an embellished and refined version of the rough fence that had been singled out for special attention at the beginning of the summer.

---

* In light of this analysis, the old hawk threat to bomb the North Vietnamese "back to the Stone Age" is ironic as it would appear that the more Stone Age a culture, the better its defenses against American might.

The Jason fence would have two separate components: an antipersonnel barrier about 20 by 100 kilometers running across the southern edge of the DMZ and into the Laotian panhandle, and an antivehicular barrier that would be twice as wide but just as long. Both would use recently developed or experimental land mines, families of small bombs, night vision devices, and electronic sensors. Both would also be serviced by aircraft that would variously patrol to collect the telling impulses given off by the various sensors, reseed the mines, and zero in to obliterate targets as they were sensed in the fence area.

Quoting directly from the report as it appears in the Gravel edition of *The Pentagon Papers*, here is how the 67 authors of the report saw their baby developing as a dynamic new weapons system:

The construction of the air-supported barrier could be initiated using currently available or nearly available components, with some necessary modifications, and could perhaps be installed by a year or so from go-ahead. However, we anticipate that the North Vietnamese would learn to cope with a barrier built this way after some period of time which we cannot estimate, but which we fear may be short. Weapons and sensors which can make a much more effective barrier, only some of which are now under development, are not likely to be available in less than 18 months to 2 years. Even these, it must be expected, will eventually be overcome by the North Vietnamese, so that further improvements in weaponry will be necessary. Thus we envisage a dynamic "battle of the barrier," in which the barrier is repeatedly improved and strengthened by the introduction of new components, and which will hopefully permit us to keep the North Vietnamese off balance by continually posing new problems for them.

This barrier is in concept not very different from what has already been suggested elsewhere; the new aspects are: the very large scale of area denial, especially mine fields kilometers deep rather than the conventional 100–200 meters; the very large numbers and persistent employment of weapons, sensors and aircraft sorties in the barrier area; and the emphasis on rapid and carefully planned incorporation of more effective weapons and sensors into the system.

To this the Jasons attached a shopping list of the items, some developed, some being developed, that would be needed, to wit:

Gravel mines—A flat three-inch square, cloth covered item that looks like a piece of ravioli. Inside are two plastic pellets, a plastic stiffener, and about 20 grams of black powder. As small and innocent as it looks, its intended application is to blow off the foot that steps on it. Gravel mines were to later come into use as "letter bombs" in the hands of international terrorists. One, for example, was used to kill the Israeli ambassador in London in 1972.

Button bomblets—Tiny aspirin-sized mines designed to make noise when stepped on rather than to injure. The idea here was that they could explode as far as 200 feet from the acoustic sensors to signal pedestrian traffic.

SADEYE/BLU-26B Cluster Bombs—Later nicknamed "guava" bombs by the Vietnamese, these one-pound, baseball-sized bombs are usually dropped in lots of 600 or more. The bomblets are released from a dispenser in such a way as to spread them across a wide area. When they hit the ground they explode sending out smaller steel balls embedded in their cases. Because of the wide area covered by a load of these, the Jason report said they would come in handy for targets of "uncertain locations."

Acoustic detectors—Land versions of the "Acoustic Sono-bouys" then being developed by the Navy to detect submarine noises.

P-2V patrol aircraft—These would be equipped for acoustic sensor listening, Gravel seeding, vectoring in strike aircraft, and infrared detection of enemy campfires.

Strike aircraft.

Photoreconnaissance aircraft.

Photo interpreters.

(Possibly) ground teams—To be used to plant mines and sensors, gather information, and harass traffic on foot trails.

While the electronic devices were somewhat complicated, the planned operation of the two barriers in the system was not. Both would use Gravel and button bomblets that when stepped on or run over would make noise that would be picked up by the audio sensors, which, in turn, would broadcast to the patrol aircraft. The patrol plane would mark the noise and order in a SADEYE strike against the area. The two systems would operate in much the same fashion except that the antipersonnel system would rely more heavily on Gravel as a weapon (as opposed to its role as a noisemaker).

The total system envisioned by the summer study group would be a heavy consumer of goods, with an annual appetite for:

240,000,000 Gravel mines
300,000,000 button bomblets
120,000 SADEYE Clusters
19,200 acoustic sensors

All of this plus the requisite aircraft (68 patrol planes, as many as 50 planes for Gravel dispensing and so forth) would cost about $800 million a year. However, since the Jasons tacked on the caveat that it was "essential" to develop new and improved explosives, sensors, and systems to process sensor signals in order to keep the enemy outfoxed, the total cost would have to be closer to a cool billion.

While the Jason group felt that the idea was the only feasible option this side of sending hundreds of thousands more Americans into the fray and that it would indeed work, they concluded their report by allowing for the fact that the North was not without its defenses and countermeasures, which would include mine sweeping, special shelter and protection against SADEYE and Gravel, finding ways to spoof sensors, beefed-up antiaircraft coverage in the barrier areas, and an end run of the system by way of the Mekong plain, Cambodia, or the sea. For this reason the scientists said that if the barrier were installed there would be need for a "greatly stepped-up" intelligence effort to keep tabs on its effectiveness.

Meanwhile, through the summer and fall of 1966, the situation on and around the DMZ was becoming more serious. North Vietnamese infiltration was getting bolder and bolder, which brought the United States closer to an even wider conflict. Not only was United States bombing in the area at a high, but American marines were occasionally operating within three miles of North Vietnam. Reflecting the fears of those indirectly involved, a report in the *Times of India* in early October wrote of "disquieting" reports of American troops moving into the DMZ while the North Vietnamese seem to be "deliberately provoking" the US to extend the land war across the 17th parallel. A few days later Joseph Alsop's column gave evidence to show that if the goal was provocation it seemed to be working. Alsop grimly wrote, "Month after month of substantial US casualties, resulting from continuous invasions across the DMZ, would start a clamor in this country for all sorts of measures that might be high in risk."

If the message was not clear earlier it could not be missed now: bombs were not stopping troops and supplies, American casualties were mounting, and a still wider land war was threatened. What that meant in terms of the Jason study was that the fence was not an idea to be toyed with or studied, but a reasonable option demanding a quick decision.

On a separate level other factors were combining to force a quick and favorable decision from McNamara. For one, the Jason study helped him articulate his increasingly negative feelings about Rolling Thunder. Another was that it was a blunt, unequivocal statement from a large number of scholars who had reached a consensus in an area that was creating wide disagreement elsewhere. Finally there was the reason that was phrased this way by the authors of the *Pentagon Papers*, ". . . [here] were recommendations from a group of America's most distinguished scientists, men who had helped the Government produce many of its most advanced technical weapons systems since the Second War and men who were not identified with the vocal academic criticism of the Administration's Vietnam policy."

Not surprisingly, McNamara moved quickly. Seven days after the initial presentation he flew to Boston for more detailed discussions with key Jasons who got him even more enthusiastic about the fence. He also asked for and got a quick reading on the idea from the Joint Chiefs and military leaders in Vietnam. General Wheeler and his Chiefs lacked McNamara's enthusiasm primarily due to their fear that funds for the barrier would have to be squeezed from important, existing programs; however, a majority did agree that development should begin as the idea had definite promise. Sharp, on the other hand, came back with an even stronger attack on the idea than he had made earlier, bluntly terming the whole concept "impracticable." It was no secret that Sharp and his running mate General Westmoreland were of one mind in the belief that the best tactic was the "unremitting" application of air and sea power on the North. They saw this as the only way to wreck the North's war-making capacity and ability to help the Viet Cong.

Despite sharp objection from the field, on September 15, 1966, McNamara appointed Lieutenant General Alfred Starbird, a highly regarded uniformed technical manager who, among other things, had supervised the nation's 1946 to 1950 atomic energy test program, to head up Joint Task Force 728 in the Directorate of Research and Engineering, which was to develop the barrier. The group, which reported directly to the secretary of defense, was to work on a "high-priority, top secret and low profile" basis—in fact the group, which was based on the grounds of the Naval Observatory on Massachusetts Avenue in Washington, was given the name Defense Communications Planning Group, a purposely misleading and innocent-sounding cover name meant to attract no attention. For that matter the group's physical location on the grounds of the Observatory near the British Embassy was also part of the camouflage in that, despite its central location in the Washington area, an old, undistinguished building set back from Embassy Row was one of the last places one would expect to find a top secret group of such importance. (Tradition and a sense of melodrama would have put it in a highly secure, remote compound in the Rockies or at the very least a hidden enclave in the bowels of the Pentagon.)

The Defense Communications Planning Group was to last for more than five years before disbanding. Before that was to happen it was to vastly expand on the Jason outline, spark an entire generation of new weapons, change the complexion of the war in Southeast Asia as well as future wars, give new direction and unity to the massive military research and development apparatus, and alter the image of war. It now appears that the DCPG was destined to have the same impact on conventional war worldwide as the Manhattan Project, which developed the first A-bomb, had on unlimited war.

THREE

Billions for Electronics

AAU, ACAD, ACOUBUOY I, ACOUBUOY II, ACOUSID II, ACOUSID III, ADAM, ADDER, ADR, ADSID I, ADSID II, ADSID III/N&S, ARFBUOY III, BASS III, BPS, COD, COMMIKE III, DART DDT, DIRID III, DSID III, EDET III, EMID III, EXIB, EXRAY, FADSID, FTA, GATE, GSID, GSR, HADDER, HAID, HANDSID I, HANDSID II, HEC III, HELOSID, HYDAD, IGNAC, IGNID, IID, ISC, LORES, LSID, MAGID II, MAGID III, MAGID T-4, MAPR, MARDS, MICROSID III, MINIMAGID, MINISID, MINISID III, MISER, MODS, MTP, NBB, NBCS, PAR, PAID, PEMID, PIRID, PME, PSEV, PSID, RABET, RFD, RFS, SARS I, SARS III, SBB, SHAID, SMS, SOSID, USD, UVID.

—*The names of the major sensing devices developed by the Defense Communications Planning Group, 1966 to 1972.*

THE GROUP

By all accounts the Defense Communications Planning Group was a very special thing, and doubly so if you were a scientist or an engineer. This testimonial from DCPG alumnus Stanley Hirsch of the MITRE Corporation is typical: "As an engineer it is what you dream about. You count yourself as extremely lucky if something like it comes along just once in your lifetime. It allowed you to be in on the birth of an idea and see it move through all its stages—design, development, prototype, testing, production—and

32

into combat in Vietnam in just about the fastest possible time which was less than a year in most cases. This is an amazing thing because in most military projects the cycles take at least seven years and the men there at the beginning are seldom around for its application." He adds with undiminished enthusiasm, "But that's just one point, everything else about it was exhilarating. For instance, everything was streamlined and there wasn't a lot of paperwork, red tape and running around getting approval for every little thing. You could work your own hours and if you felt that you had to go to Europe, California, Vietnam or wherever to get your work done, you'd just get on the next plane. What a wonderful experience it was!"

Other DCPG alumni also talk about the organization in reverential and enthusiastic terms. Again and again comparisons are made to the Manhattan and Polaris projects, which respectively yielded the first atomic bomb and nuclear submarine. Both have become legends, especially to scientists and engineers, in terms of their pace, daring, level of excitement, and freedom from bureaucratic Mickey Mouse. Besides the specific points that Hirsch makes, others recall these extras: the conscious awareness of being present at a turning point in the technology of warfare . . . being a charter member in a new technological fraternity, what has come to be known as the sensor community . . . being given extraordinary rights to spend money and "task" the services—that is to assign work to regular military organizations on the highest priority basis. On this latter point a former project member says, "If DCPG said it needed 10,000 chocolate cream pies from the Army by noon the next day, it would get them and without any questions. Having such rights annoyed others no end."

When the truly extraordinary nature of this group was spelled out for the public record four years after its founding, no exaggeration in these recollections was found. At that public accounting, a 1970 investigation into the Electronic Battlefield

Program by the Senate Armed Services Committee, DCPG's director termed the group's situation "unique and unprecedented." Beyond those privileges already recalled, this claim was based on such rights, arrangements and resources as direct access to the secretary of defense for broad policy and funding decisions as well as freedom to contact any part of the military up to and including the Joint Chiefs for whatever reason; the right to jump immediately to the "head of the line" for materials, facilities, and contractors; the freedom to tap scientific help in government agencies outside the Defense Department; and virtually unlimited funding.

However, what is unarguably the most graphic piece of information about the DCPG came to light during those same hearings in the fall of 1970 as a footnote to its funding. The piece of information was that DCPG had been given $678 million that it never bothered to use—that is, money in addition to what it spent. These excess millions were not returned to the Treasury but passed along to the Army, Navy, and Air Force to use for whatever they saw fit. To put this into another context, the DCPG surplus was almost four times the federal cancer research budget for fiscal 1970. There is more to this story that we will come back to later, but the fact remains that for each of the members of the DCPG team there was over $3 million in appropriated dollars to be consumed elsewhere.

Such wealth and power, however, were not exactly what was envisioned at the very beginning because according to the script that was written by the Jason Division the job at hand was essentially to integrate off-the-shelf hardware into a system (albeit with a few modifications and pieces of new equipment here and there), train some operators, and ship it all to Southeast Asia. The outline was wrong. David R. Israel, a MITRE Corporation employee brought in as one of the original scientific advisors, explains: ". . . the effort immediately became much more difficult than had been anticipated—we started with existing acoustic

tic sensors and their associated communications, for instance, and immediately had problems. The equipment was not suitable for the combination of air-delivered, ground-emplaced, and long-range transmission—and we needed all three features. It became clear that substantial developmental and engineering activities were required involving sensors, aerial delivery, accurate navigation and position location, sensor monitoring equipment, data processing and display devices, and a wide variety of mines and munitions. There was a huge job ahead of us."

To tackle the job, an Engineering Directorate was quickly formed for DCPG composed of highly qualified people brought in from the services, Civil Service, and private high-technology groups close to government. For instance, the aforementioned MITRE Corporation, a think tank spin-off from MIT, which since its founding in 1958 has done most of its work for the Air Force, supplied more than 50 professionals while the Sandia Corporation, a research adjunct of Western Electric with expertise in seismics, supplied another relatively large group. In short, a classic interdisciplinary team was needed and quickly fielded with people with backgrounds in specific, and as often as not esoteric, areas such as signal processing logic, antijamming techniques and acoustics. MITRE's Dr. Casper L. Woodbridge, now the company's associate department head for sensor systems applications, says, "In scientific and engineering terms what was created in a very few weeks was a new community, the sensing community. For this reason alone, DCPG has historic importance."

For its first goal, DCPG decided to develop the air-delivered predominently antivehicular barrier outlined by the Jasons as one of the two components of the overall system. During what one veteran of the effort terms "a 10-month burst of collective creative energy," the first prototype was ready for testing at Eglin Air Force Base in Florida. Although it was soon to be rendered crude by further DCPG innovation, the collection of equipment—mostly newly invented—set for testing at Eglin in mid–1967 was considerably more sophisticated and ambitious than the Jasons had originally ordered. Among other features, the first system employed acoustic, seismic, magnetic, and infrared sensors to detect the enemy—not just the acoustic sensors on the Jasons' list.

In July 1967 during the Florida tests when the effort was still most secret, there was a nightmarish blunder that subjected American civilians to an element of the system. More than 5,000 button bomblets—the aspirin-sized explosives that when stepped on make a loud noise that could be picked up by acoustic sensors at considerable distances—being used in trials at Eglin got washed away from the base during the torrential rains of a sudden storm and into Choctawhatchie Bay from which large numbers were washed ashore onto the crowded local beaches. The problem became public when Donald Spinelli of Fort Walton Beach found one and tried to pry it open with his fingers. It exploded and he was treated for hand and eye injuries. This and the fact that more and more bomblets were washing ashore forced the military to abandon its secret efforts at recovery. On July 16, a Sunday, most of the 10,000 people on the 120 miles of bay beaches were asked to leave, with those in the "most dangerous areas" actually being escorted away by the military. Completing the odd scene was a plane circling overhead with a loudspeaker broadcasting warnings. The worst moment during the incident came when an Air Force demolition expert was blinded while moving a box of several hundred bomblets that exploded. Through all of this, the only thing the Air Force would say was that the devices were part of a "highly sensitive" project.

Nor was that all that went awry during DCPG's early days. For the simple reason that any and all ideas were welcome, some exotic schemes found their way into the hopper. One that soared for a time was the plan to train munitions-carrying pigeons to land on North Vietnamese trucks where they would explode on touchdown as a special triggering device reacted to metal. While most everyone contacted from DCPG remembers the project and that it stopped abruptly, there are several different versions of why it stopped. It would appear that one or more of these reasons ended project pigeon:

(1) It was discovered that pigeons could not be taught to distinguish a communist from a noncommunist truck.

(2) That it feared the labor intensive North Vietnamese economy would have much more time for things like pigeon training and all sorts of countermeasures would quickly follow. For example, a Red pigeon might intercept an American one and escort it to the nearest parked helicopter (which could only be American or South Vietnamese).

(3) That even if the program was minimally successful it would not be worth the ultimate flack it would attract when made public, especially from organized anticruelty to animal groups and the press, which one participant says would have immediately termed a "birdbrained" idea.

Then there was the so-called Lava plan to find the right chemical mixture that could be dropped on the Ho Chi Minh Trail and turn the damp soil to grease (the right mixture was never found). And there was a vaguely recalled plan to use dogs as sensors and another that somehow remotely kept tabs on certain bacteria that responded to the presence of human beings.

While these ideas and others like them died on the DCPG drawing board or in the early mock-up phase, the award for the most outlandish would have to go to one that went all the way to the hardware stage and into the field.* Let MITRE Corporation

* Anyone collecting bizarre weapons, weapons concepts, and associated equipment will find the Vietnam era to be an especially fertile time for such things. In researching this book the author was struck by these three developments among others: (1) An Army effort to develop a "super seed" to be dropped from planes in vast quantities to create barriers with "high obstacle potential" around missile sites and airfields. Oddly, work on these specially treated seeds began in 1968 while the nation was deeply involved in a vast defoliation effort. Perhaps, by some twist of the military imagination, "foliation" could somehow offset the side effects of military defoliation. (2) A RAND Corporation study proposing a "Flash Bulb" approach to night fighting. Envisioned were gigantic flash bulbs that would be so powerful that they would thwart enemy night operations because they

engineer Stanley Hirsch, formerly of DCPG, describe this one in his own words: "Did you hear about the sensor we came up with in the shape of a dog turd? Well, it was about the size of your thumb and really looked like a turd. We figured that they'd be good on the Ho Chi Minh Trail where trucks and troops would make contact with them. These were contact sensors, by the way, that would give off a small impulse when stepped on or run over and a larger device would pick up that impulse and relay it. We called it TURDSID because it was a Seismic Intrusion Detector or SID. There was one big problem with it, however, and that was that after a lot of work had gone into it we discovered that there weren't any dogs running around on the Ho Chi Minh Trail so it was later reconfigured to look like a small piece of wood."

TURDSIDS aside, the first barrier system was put into operation in Southeast Asia in the latter part of 1967 as the heart of a special operation with the code name Igloo White.* This was slightly more than a year from the day when DCPG began. Right behind this first system was the second, which was designed to cut personnel infiltration. However, before this system could be installed as intended along the DMZ, the Tet Offensive of January, 1968 and, more to the point, the siege of American forces at Khe Sanh intervened to cause a critical change in plans. But both the Igloo White operation and what happened at Khe Sanh take us a bit ahead of our story. First, let us pause to appreciate the novel, prophetic, and often horrific handiwork of DCPG and its helpers.

---

could cause substantial periods of flash blindness or damage the retina. (3) Finally, there was an effort to use bedbugs on enemy troops. As the story has been recalled, a batch of aggressive bedbugs were dropped on a suspected NVA regiment; the bedbugs, however, were unable to make the needed political and military decisions and the result caused considerable scratching of American heads and bodies.

* Igloo White is a code word to remember; however, the same cannot be said for most of the many others that DCPG's efforts inspired. They may have confused outsiders as they were supposed to but they also confused many participants who, then as now, got Dutch Door, Illinois City, Duffel Bag, Duel Blade, Dye Marker, Muscle Shoals, and others mixed up.

THE BEEP AND THE BOOM

The one "success" of the American side of the debacle in Southeast Asia was the advancement of military technology. Great advances were spurred in such areas as solid state electronics, ordnance, and helicopters, which were perfected as battlefield workhorses to the point that the Chinese are now talking about buying them from us. Old-fashioned dumb bombs gave way to laser- and TV-guided "smart" ones and the computer metamorphosed from a lesser military tool into a major element of all sophisticated weapons systems. What was done by DCPG directly and that which it sponsored or inspired elsewhere in the national weapons development apparatus are a perfect case in point—in fact, a good deal of the rest of this book will be spent illustrating why it may also be the most important case in point. Reduced to its absolutes this technology boils down to one that some military men have come to call that of the "beep and the boom."

The beep was provided by many classes of instruments but none more important than sensors, developed by DCPG, used to remotely "feel" the presence of an enemy. The basic elements of these sensors and those that have come along since then are a detecting unit, electronic logic circuit, radio transmitter, and a battery. Simply, whatever kind of disturbance the sensor is set to detect is converted into an electrical signal. The internal logic of the sensor determines if this signal is a valid possibility or a false alarm, and if it appears to be real the radio transmitter is switched on and the signal passed along to those monitoring it some distance away. The most common military sensors and those that were given top priority by DCPG were acoustic and seismic sensors.

Seismic sensors are intended to detect the disturbance in the ground caused by a person walking or a vehicle passing. While the geology of an area and the sophistication of the sensor determine the range of detection, picking up footsteps 30 yards away, or a car or truck at more than 300 yards, are average. The most common first generation seismic sensors are the PSID (Patrol Seismic Intrusion Detector), a small unit placed by hand, and ADSID (Air-Delivered Seismic Intrusion Detector), which are dropped from high-speed aircraft to embed themselves in the ground. Acoustic sensors are listening devices that come in handy in conjunction with seismic sensors to confirm a target. One DCPG innovation, ACOUSID (ACOUstic/Seismic Intrusion Detector), combined both. One of the most popular early model acoustic sensors is the ACOUBUOY (or Acoustic Buoy), which can be dropped from planes into the jungle where its parachute would normally catch in the dense foliage where it would stay to listen for truck and troop movement until its battery ran down.

Other early models detect electromagnetic field disturbance or react to magnetic materials. An example of the former would be EMID (Electromagnetic Intrusion Detector), which sets up a radio field around itself and flashes a warning when that field is broken by a moving object. One of the latter is MAGID (MAGnetic Intrusion Detector), which reacts to a rifle, truck, or other magnetic object moving by. In Southeast Asia, the MAGID was almost always attached to a small seismic intrusion detector called the MINISID and wired in such a way that both seismic and magnetic activation were needed to send out notice of a target. Presumably, this tandem configuration would distinguish a man from a man with a gun and a truck from a water buffalo.

Not all of the sensors that worked in the lab worked in the jungle, so some were lost along the way like the PIRID (Passive Infrared Intrusion Detector), which was intended to sense fine temperature changes in its field of view allowing it to "count" the warm bodies passing by. In the field all sorts of problems bedevilled the PIRID including an unexplained tendency for it to attract insects, which threw it out of whack.

In addition to this important basic family of remote sensors, there were scores of new electronic targeting, surveillance, and computing devices that were brought together to function in conjunction with the sensors. Some came right out of DCPG, others were ordered by DCPG, and a number had already been developed or were under development as DCPG came along and fit nicely into the electronic package. Indeed a whole gaggle of new organizations and systems—complete with a raft of new acronyms (REMBASS, STANO, MASSTER, BISS and more)— were created to develop and refine this ambitious new technology in DCPG's wake. There will be more on these satellite efforts later, but they are mentioned here to demonstrate that there were hundreds more involved in the effort than DCPG's size alone would indicate.

The hardware list is long but three specific types of equipment serve to give the flavor of the motley line:

People Sniffers—These pieces of equipment, which are more properly designated Aircraft Mounted Concealed Personnel Detector, were built to pick up ammonia in human sweat and urine as well as engine exhaust. Their origin is unexpected: as *Chemistry* magazine reported in 1972, "People sniffers were developed for the food industry as an outgrowth of attempts to monitor taste appeal of processed foods by machines." In the flesh these nasal radars look like variations on the design of the common tank type home vacuum cleaner and come complete with a long hose, which in war hangs from the helicopter or whatever is carrying it to draw in odors for analysis. Although they had their share of early problems and drawbacks—for instance, cattle and decomposing human flesh gave off the same signal as live humans and they could not tell how many people were there when they did find live targets—they did become widely used tactical helpers, especially in the war's second half. *Ordnance* magazine reviewed them so: "Sniffers installed in Huey helicopters combed the Vietnamese countryside and proved invaluable in detecting the unseen enemy. American field commanders used them exclusively as a method for gaining contact with the enemy, and the devices were credited with locating numerous cache sites." Apparently that was not good enough for some. An American officer told *Christian Science Monitor* reporter Beverly Deepe late in 1968, "When the Army comes up with a model that will tell us the difference between the goodies and the baddies, then the 'people sniffer' will win the war for us."

The Starlight Scope—Overall, it was the most widely used detecting device of the Vietnam war. It magnifies existing star or moonlight up to 50,000 times, which in real terms means that with the help of one of the bigger, better scopes, a soldier can get a bead on a target more than a half-mile away in dim, night light. Even the smallest version, which fits onto the stock of a M-16 rifle, gives a GI night vision out to 400 or so yards. Starlight scopes per se are just one type of new equipment intended to roll back the night. In Vietnam many aircraft were outfitted with special low-light level TV cameras for picking up targets in the dark. A special one-two-punch night vision system was to be found in the INFANT system (for Iroquois Night Fighter and Night Tracker), which was a helicopter sporting both a low-light level TV and an image intensification system like the one found in the starlight scope. Then there are the closely related thermal-imaging night vision devices that sense temperature differentials both at night and through fog.*

Ground Target Radars—To show that all the acquisition and surveillance equipment pressed into service for Southeast Asia was not new or exotic, an important class of item in the overall collection were small ground target radars that were not too

---

* On at least one occasion the military resorted to rather raw show biz to show off its new see-in-the-dark devices. Orville Schell wrote in *Earth* magazine that the Starlight Scopes were introduced to the press at a special presentation in which reporters used Scopes to watch a skit in a blackened room. At one point in the skit one black kimonoed "Viet Cong" dropped the kimono revealing a shapely woman in a bathing suit. Schell quotes this from *Air Force* magazine, "Details of the face and dress were plainly visible, attested to by the audience whistles when the kimono dropped. . . ."

different from the older and larger models that saw service in Korea. The importance of these radars was their ability to pick up occasional blips moving through the stationary blips given off by trees, rocks, and houses.

There are more too, but the point has been established that the "beep" (bleep, blip, and whatever) came in all shapes, sizes, and configurations—a far cry from the single acoustic sensor the Jasons had ordered. Now to the "boom."

So too, while the Jasons had envisioned relying on a single one-two-punch of two antipersonnel weapons (SADEYE cluster bombs and Gravel mines), the munitions collection soon grew much larger. Some items already existed and were taken off the shelf as they were or were especially modified for the system, while others were developed exclusively for the electronic battlefield. In very short order, the two items in the Jason rough outline had become more than a score in DCPG's quiver. Their variety was such that individual devices that went bump in the night ranged in weight from a mere, maiming 0.7 ounces to an earthshaking 15,000 pounds.

On the smaller side were such as the aforementioned tea bag-sized Gravel mine and the new Dragontooth and WAAPM mines. The Dragontooth is a tiny jagged object that is so small that it can be packed in lots of 4,800 to a dispenser. The type of dispenser used for this and other small antipersonnel weapons looks like a normal bomb casing with the major difference that it splits in half, pea pod style, in mid-air, allowing its contents to spread out over a large area. It means getting ahead of our story for a moment but the best way to get an idea of Dragontooth's reason for being is to quote from the 1970 Senate Armed Services Committee hearings on the electronic battlefield for this exchange between Senator Barry Goldwater and an Air Force ordnance expert, Major Anderson:

GOLDWATER: "How much damage can the Dragontooth do?"
ANDERSON: "How much damage, sir?"

GOLDWATER: "Yes, how much damage?"

ANDERSON: "It is purely anti-personnel. If a person steps on it, it could blow his foot off. If a truck rolls over it, it won't blow the tire."

Then we have the imaginative DCPG original WAAPM, or Wide Area Antipersonnel Mine, which at first looks like the baseball-sized SADEYE or "guava" bomblet. However, when WAAPM hits the ground wires shoot out for several feet in all directions, which is why the Vietnamese called them "spider" bombs. Who or whatsoever disturbs one of the wires causes the mine to detonate, shooting fragmentation pellets for about 200 feet. WAAPM came in at least two versions, the BLU-42 that exploded on the ground and the more ambitious BLU-54, a "bounding" mine that pops into the air before exploding thereby increasing its destructive range. WAAPMs were designed to be packed 18 to the cannister, which, in turn, were packed 10 to a dispenser—or 180 to a lot. Their odd-looking but aerodynamically sound shape allowed them to flutter in the airstream, thereby dispensing them over a wide area.

At the furthest end of the spectrum from the 0.7-ounce Dragontooth mine is the BLU-82/B general purpose bomb, which is now the nation's heaviest air-delivered conventional weapon. It has been variously nicknamed the "Daisy Cutter," "Big Blue 82," and the "Cheeseburger." It is $4\frac{1}{2}$ feet in diameter, over 11 feet long, and 12,600 pounds of its total weight is a special blasting agent (DBA-22M) consisting of an aqueous mix of ammonium nitrate, aluminium powder, and a binder, a formulation which, according to biologist Arthur W. Westing, who studied the weapon's environmental effects firsthand in Vietnam, ". . . provides a concussive blast surpassed only by that of a nuclear bomb." The immediate father of the Daisy Cutter is the 10,000 pound Second World War "blockbuster." Some blockbusters, which had been in storage since the 1940s, were used in experiments in Vietnam beginning in 1967 as a means of creating instant clearings in the dense jungle. Success, especially in creating clear helicopter assault areas, led to the development and introduction of the present weapon in 1970.

Daisy Cutters are delivered from cargo planes by parachute and are detonated just a few feet above the ground for best effect. Their radial blast leaves no crater but still clears *all* trees, underbrush, and whatever to produce a perfectly bald spot about the size of a football field. While most Daisy Cutters used in Southeast Asia were employed in what the Air Force termed "explosive bulldozers," their awesome power soon found new applications against storage areas, interdiction routes, antiaircraft installations, and truck parks. While Westing was in Vietnam trying to determine the ecological impact of this weapon he had a hard time getting biological data from the Air Force, but had no trouble getting enthusiastic endorsements for it. One officer called it "a super bomb with a super punch" while a senior 7th Air Force commander explained, ". . . they have such a devastating effect that we hate to give them much publicity." The last American application of the Big Blue 82 in Southeast Asia (one hopes) came during the American Marine invasion of Tang Island during President Ford's *Mayaguez* incident when one was dropped on an area believed to be harboring Cambodian troops. It was said to have taken considerable pressure off the hard-pressed Marines.

Between the extremes of Dragontooth and Daisy Cutter were a number of others including such old standbys as napalm and white phosphorus, horrific bits of pyrotechnology about which much has been written. Less well known but just as, if not more lethal, are a class of weapons known as cluster bombs. They were first used in the Second World War when the military discovered that a large number of small bomblets were often much more effective than a few large bombs of equal collective power. It was not, however, until Vietnam that the cluster bombs came into their own as carriers for items ranging from CS-1 tear gas to flechettes, an apt term for steel darts whose prime function is to shred human flesh or pin people to trees. CBUs—as the Air Force commonly refers to its cluster bomb units—were in use before DCPG came along but funding and encouragement from that group sped up their development and increased their use considerably. Besides the CBU bomblet the Vietnamese called "guava" because of its similarity to that fruit, there are also the "pineapple" and "orange" (more formally, these are respectively the BLU-66 and BLU-24 bomblets with BLU standing for Bomb, Live Unit). Pineapples are loaded into dispensers in lots of 360. Their shape, cylindrical with fins coming out of the top like pineapple leaves, causes them to land nose first and the shock of impact causes 250 small steel balls to shoot out on all sides. The orange, on the other hand, is an especially ingenious adaptation to the jungle environment. Because of special vanes attached to it, the bomblet spins very fast while falling. It is set to explode only when it slows to a speed of less than 2,000 RPM, which happens when it hits the jungle canopy making it explode beneath the canopy where, of course, the people are.

Then there were items like BLU-31, a 700-pound land mine that buries itself in the ground to explode when a vehicle passes, and its first cousin the MK-36 "Destructor," an antivehicular bomb triggered to go off when a moving object of a predetermined size gets near it. If a commander wishing to clear a large area happened to run out of Daisy Cutters there was always Pave Pat II, a 2,500 pound pressurized propane bomb set to explode above the jungle canopy. And there were some interesting hybrids in the collection such as the M-36, which combines cluster and incendiary bomb technologies. Each M-36 opened to release 182 individually wrapped incendiary bombs.

From a purely technological point of view (and perhaps historical point of view too) no type of bomb sent overseas could compare in importance to the new "smart" bombs that the United States first used in quantity in March 1972 on targets in North Vietnam. These bombs come in two types: laser-guided versions that home in on a target that has been illuminated by a laser beam, and the electro-optical or TV-guided glide bomb, which is literally shown a target and then keeps its "eye" on it right up until it hits. Both types proved to be much more accurate than their primitive free-fall predecessors and for this reason the military claims they are much more economical. For instance, the official Air Force claim for its laser-guided smart bombs is that one can be as effective as 100 conventional bombs at 10 percent the cost. One popular smarty is the HOBO (HOming BOmb) System. Its manufacturer, North American Rockwell, calls it a "launch-and-forget" system because the pilot can forget the TV-bomb once he has picked a target and released the bomb. The bomb is gliding in towards its target as the pilot is escaping. HOBO and most other smart bombs are created by bolting on special modules to existing dumb bombs. In Southeast Asia, conventional bombs ranging in size from 300 to 3,000 pounds were turned into highly accurate guided weapons. In terms of the technology of bombs, even conservative experts in the field term this development a revolutionary one.

Between these beeps and booms, of course, was all the ancillary electronic equipment that tied them together—relay gear, monitoring systems, antennae, computers, communications equipment of all sorts, beep-collecting and boom-delivering aircraft, and the like—so the total package was collectively enormous.

THE PUBLIC LINE

Meanwhile, back in the outside world, word of the barrier began seeping out although this early talk was of a conventional nonelectronic barbed wire and mine affair. As far back as August 1, 1966, when the Jasons were just getting down to work, columnists Rowland Evans and Robert Novak reported that the Pentagon was seriously studying an anti-infiltration barricade across the southern edge of the DMZ. Then, in early October two reporters, Jim Lucas of Scripps-Howard and Charles Mohr of *The New York Times*, each filed stories on the concept from Vietnam, which proved to be right on target save for still missing its electronic content. Lucas even went so far as to correctly report that the system McNamara was dishing up was going to cost an estimated billion dollars. Mohr's dispatch, among other things, said that McNamara (then in Vietnam) was reportedly annoyed by the fact that mention of the barrier had appeared in the press.

As discussion of a barrier system continued to appear in the press through the fall and winter of 1966 and 1967, McNamara and other Pentagon leaders expressed outward coolness to the idea, only admitting that they would look into it, even though they were already deeply committed to a barrier. Meanwhile, as frustration with the bombing grew, others embraced the barrier idea as their own. Senate Majority Leader Mike Mansfield became intrigued with the idea of a physical barrier along the 17th parallel and openly pushed for one as an alternative to bombing. On the other hand, Henry Cabot Lodge, then ambassador to South Vietnam, was plumping for a barrier that would run west from Saigon to the jut in Cambodia known as the Parrot's Beak, which he felt would reduce enemy troops and supplies coming out of Cambodia and the Mekong Delta. Then, on March 20, 1967, when President Johnson went to Guam for a strategy conference on the war, Premier Nguyen Cao Ky and a delegation of South Vietnamese leaders presented a "radical" new proposal for controlling infiltration from the North: a hundred mile long "fortified" line. (One of the Vietnamese leaders told R.W. Apple, reporting from Guam for *The New York Times*, that if the line was not built, "You will be faced with a war that could last 20 years.")

Then, on April 15 Premier Ky announced in a speech at Bien Hoa that work had just begun on a "fortified barrier zone" and that some 20,000 peasants would soon be evacuated from hamlets in the area. Reports on the clearing operation would continue for some months. By summer, for instance, it would be reported that a 600-yard strip had already been cleared inland from the sea for 10 miles and that it would be pushed westward for another 13 miles.

Two days after the Ky announcement the other shoe dropped as the ever so important electronic nature of the system finally came out with *Newsweek*'s Periscope section providing the nation with the first clear picture of what was happening in an April 17 item entitled "An Electronic Picket Line at the DMZ." It correctly described a new array of automated sensors that were being readied for actual use across the 17th parallel.* In short order, others were assembling the picture and anyone willing to splice together what appeared piecemeal in various general military and trade magazines and newspapers over the next few months would have come up with an accurate outline. Despite this and the fact that the information was coming right from the Pentagon with "off the record" and "not for attribution" provisos attached, the official word on an attributable basis on all questions about an electronic fence was a "no comment," or worse. One of the most amusing denials was made in a June letter to Senator Carl T. Curtis who had written to the Pentagon on behalf of an old friend, constituent, and barrier advocate who wanted to know where the idea stood. None other than Lieutenant General Marvin L. McNickle, the number two man at the Office of Department of Defense Research and Engineering (DDR&E), called it an interesting idea worthy of study but not one that was in the cards for the time being. Rather than just leave it at that, he went on to detail specific reasons such as, "Reallocation of effort to construction of a barrier in this very difficult terrain would seriously

---

* After this nearly perfect opening, a follow-up June Periscope item claimed that the electronic systems would require 250,000 mobile troops to respond to its alarms. Even moderate numbers of troops were never considered for use with the electronic system that had as one of its central selling points the fact that it would bring wholesale troop reductions.

penalize military and pacification actions in more immediately threatened areas."

The current entree, of course, became a specialty of the house during the Johnson administration, variously called trial ballooning and judging the wind. In this case the outline of a Model-T electronic battlefield was, on one hand, being leaked to see if it attracted flak from Congress, press, and public; and, on the other, officially denied so that it could be held back if the flak was too heavy. With this particular item there was no problem.

By the late summer of 1967, the time was ripe for an announcement. There was increasingly strong public, Congressional, and editorial frustration expressed with the war in general and the DMZ in particular. The grim irony of a zone created to keep peace between the two Vietnams was that it had become the bloodiest of all sites for American troops, a place that *Time* termed "a running sore." As had been the case for some two years, United States Marines were suffering heavy casualties from an opponent able to cross, strike from, and jump back over an imaginary line that Americans were not allowed to get too near let alone cross. Not only was there this particular situation but also the prospect that the whole conflict would never stop escalating. The President had made an August announcement to the effect that he was going to commit another 50,000 men, bringing the total to 525,000. Besides all of this, the press and Congress wanted the project officially confirmed and described in greater detail.

So on September 7, 1967, McNamara himself called a press conference to confirm that a plan was indeed underway to create a 47 mile long barrier across South Vietnam just south of the DMZ and that it would rely on equipment ranging from barbed wire to highly sophisticated electronic detectors. He said little more than that and then immediately forbade all discussion of the scheme by the military, its civilian employees, and contractors. As he put it, "The more the enemy knows about our plans, the more ready he could be to defeat the system once it is installed." After a year of speculation and leaks, the actual McNamara briefing was distinctly anticlimactic; its aftermath was not.

For most of the rest of the fall the barrier became a topic for conversation, further speculation, and debate, which for the most was conducted in a decidedly upbeat and, well, hopeful tone. McNamara had given an already war-weary nation a rather startling but easily understood initiative that implied an earlier end to the war or at least the opportunity to cut back on troop levels. In the abstract at least, the grubby, bloody, and altogether questionable foreign excursion that had turned into the most unpopular war in American history was given its first bit of technological glamor appropriate to a nation two summers away from a manned moon landing. The fence was clearly something special. Among other distinctions, it fell into the rarest class of military programs: an idea deemed so important that it merited a crash development program during a war for application in that war, like the A-bomb and radar before it.

In the discussion process, the plan picked up a slew of new nicknames—McNamara's Wall, De Fence (a pun used more by the military than outsiders), the Strip, McNamara's Fairway, and more—but the one that stuck was the McNamara Line.

For their part, editorial page writers gave it some relatively good early reviews. *The Christian Science Monitor* and *Philadelphia Bulletin* said it was an experiment good enough for a full trial while *The Baltimore Sun* deemed it "eminently sensible." *The Washington Post* considered it worthwhile as it had benefits beyond hindering infiltration, which included political and psychological ones—for instance, it would dramatize the essentially defensive character of operations in the South. Of course others were not quite as sanguine. *The Washington Star* felt it could work but only if strung into Laos where a DMZ-only system would be outflanked. "It is tragic but true," said *The Dallas News* in one of the few really negative editorial comments, "that the ultimate task of turning back a determined aggressor cannot be left to masonry or barbed wire or to any other static barrier. It is a task that must finally be done by men."

To some the barrier was a notion that separated the doves and moderates from the probombing hawks favoring an even wider air war. For instance, Chalmers Roberts of *The Washington Post* pointed out in his analysis that if it worked it would allow the US to stop bombing and thereby pave the way to the negotiating table, which would not sit well with the crowd that was in favor of closing Haiphong with bombs and similar escalations. "In short," he concluded, "the DMZ barrier may serve to outflank the hawks." In line with this analysis, hawkish Senator John Tower of Texas expressed concern for the "static policies it signifies" and Evans and Novak reported that the two members of the Joint Chiefs of Staff opposed to the McNamara Line were the two most responsible for bombing, General John P. McConnell of the Air Force and Admiral Thomas H. Moorer of the Navy.

McNamara's order to remain mum was immediately disobeyed by both those hot and cool to the system who, with news of it now out in the open, wanted to have their views registered. Those taken with its potential achievements came out of their corner bragging about its coming importance. "I think it is really our secret weapon," said Charles M. Herzfeld, former director of the Advanced Research Projects Office in a typical comment. Another faction was lukewarm, such as the Army general who told *Time*, "I guess it can't hurt anything, if it doesn't draw men and resources away from something important." *Navy Times* columnist Gene Famiglietti found some military men who were objecting outright for reasons ranging from its economic price to the belief that it was "militarily unwise."

After the initial flurry of interest died down at the beginning of the winter of 1967 and 1968, little attention was paid to the scheme for several months. In December the Pentagon made a terse announcement to the effect that part of the system was in place. However, in the spring reports began appearing in the press to the effect that the barrier was either (a) not working, (b) way behind in schedule and not complete, (c) about to be or already abandoned or (d) all of the above. In March *US News & World Report* pointed out that the McNamara Line was in deep trouble and told of the skepticism about it in the field turning to cynicism, and a *New York Times* piece by Gene Roberts with a Vietnamese dateline went into great detail about the apparent demise of the system, specifically reporting ". . . no evidence of any work on the line for many weeks, and no indication that any effort is under way to speed construction of the multimillion dollar project." Even more pointed was a May Associated Press dispatch entitled "$1 Billion 'McNamara Wall' Fizzles" which said it "leaked" to the extent that between 80,000 and 100,000 North Vietnamese had been able to move through it since the beginning of the year.

Before long, the McNamara Line had become still another symbol of the war's ongoing failure. In a summer, 1968 column, Mary McGrory, in making a Buchwaldian case for sending the Chicago Police Force, fresh from its "victory" at the Democratic National Convention, to Vietnam, said, "The McNamara electronic fence at the border has either never been constructed or never worked. Why not set up Mayor Daley's elaborate barriers— his electronic pass machines, his guards and his ushers?" She added, "Any ordinary North Vietnamese, no matter how filled with revolutionary spirit or Communist fervor, would turn around and go home rather than go through what the delegates to the national convention had to suffer to get to their appointed places." Others went further in deriding the system. For example, a *Washington Daily News* editorial entitled "McNamara's Folly" opened by comparing it to the Edsel and worked up to making the point that when McNamara makes a mistake it is bound to be a "lulu" and the costs astronomical.

Finally in March, 1969, just about a year after all of the talk about the failure of the McNamara Line had begun circulating,

Defense Secretary Melvin Laird said in his first "posture" report to Congress that it had been cancelled because ". . . it did not work out as expected."

The program hardly needed a formal cancellation notice as the press was right in reporting that it had begun to flounder many months before. Indeed, it had never even been fully installed. A number of reasons contributed to this, including early evidence that the barrier would be subject to massive end running (as many had predicted), opposition to the idea by field commanders, early experience with the use of decoy groups at one point who would be deployed to divert attention from larger groups crossing at another, and more. But all of the specific reasons pretty much fit into one larger general idea, which was that no matter how good the idea looked on paper in Washington, it was a linear idea not meant for a 360-degree war.

However, the military was not abandoning the concepts inherent in the McNamara Line, but instead began expanding on them. A greater idea now expanded the fence to become far more flexible and mobile—all the gadgetry could be moved to wherever it was most needed. As we are about to see, the McNamara Line did not so much die as it became the "Westmoreland Umbrella," opening across South Vietnam and into Laos, Cambodia, and Thailand. Ironically, after the Laird cancellation statement when there was no shortage of glib obituaries for the original scheme, its second incarnation was not only thriving but had moved well into the "billion dollars spent" category. One who was certainly not missing what was going on was the Line's namesake who, a few days before stepping down as secretary of defense, had been asked by a member of the House Appropriations Committee what had ever become of the so-called McNamara Line? "The McNamara Line is no longer referred to as that because it is successful," McNamara replied.

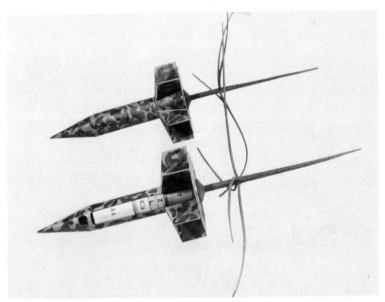

JUNGLE PLANT. The latest versions of the ADSID (Air Delivered Seismic Intrusion Detector). This popular device was used extensively in Southeast Asia to detect men and vehicles and features two special elements: a destruct mechanism that destroys it if someone tries to open it, and a design that allows it to be chucked from a jet to be embedded in the ground. The part that remains above ground is a green antenna resembling a weed. (U.S. Army)

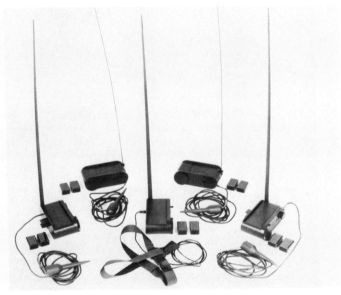

SENSOR SET. A seismic sensor system used by small patrols for ambush and counter-ambush operations. The item in the center is a receiver and the other four are PSIDs (Patrol Seismic Intrusion Detectors). The spikelike objects attached to each set is a geophone that is buried in the ground to sense seismic disturbances. (U.S. Army)

TRUCK KILLER. An Air Force AC-130 in flight over Vietnam. This special plane acted as the prime "aerial battleship" in the Igloo White operation over the Ho Chi Minh Trail. Shortly after the plane was introduced the Air Force claimed that one had knocked out 68 enemy trucks in less than an hour. (U.S. Air Force)

NERVE CENTER. The computer-packed Infiltration Surveillance Center in Thailand from which the Igloo White operation against traffic on the Ho Chi Minh Trail was managed. The building itself was reputedly the largest in Southeast Asia. (U.S. Air Force)

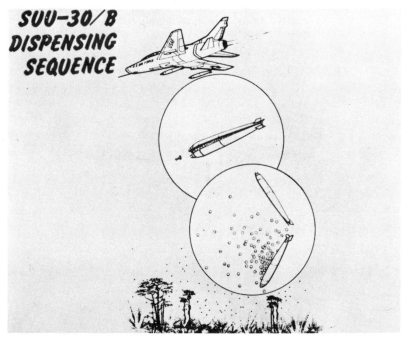

GUAVA. Air Force rendering of how "guava" bomblets were dispensed over Southeast Asia. The plane released a special "clam shell" type dispenser that opens in midair sending the bomblets over a wide area. The exploding balls—665 in each dispenser—were primarily used in Vietnam as an antipersonnel weapon. (U.S. Air Force)

SENSORY AWARENESS. A recorder that marks sensor activations allows detection of movement to be graphically displayed. The operator here is attempting to interpret "enemy" movement during exercises at Fort Hood, Texas. (C. H. Reynolds, MITRE)

DISPENSER. The latest in sensor delivery is this special dispenser shown here mounted under an F-4 capable of precisely ejecting up to 16 sensors in a single pass. Other new delivery techniques for sensors include firing them to their desired location in an artillery shell and dropping them from RPVs (Remotely Piloted Aircraft). (U.S. Navy/MITRE)

CAMOUFLAGE. A number of means of making sensors unobtrusive have been invented including these for war in Europe. (U.S. Navy/MITRE)

WATCH YOUR STEP. One of the many new sensor set-ups that are part of the current electronic battlefield. Here noiseless button bomblets (NBBS), which are disguised as such things as twigs and animal droppings, are activated when a human walks close by. The NBB sends a signal to an ARFBUOY transmitter, which passes the signal along to those in charge of the action. (U.S. Navy/MITRE)

AAU/MINISID

PAID/MINISID

COMBO. Artist's rendering of GIs setting up a set of sensors in the field. The MINISID seismic detectors shown here are usually used in combination with magnetic sensors, a parlay that the military believes will go a long way in helping it discriminate between targets. The seismic sensor notifies monitoring stations that someone is out there moving and the magnetic detector tells if that person is moving with something metal such as a rifle. What the military has not made clear is how a magnetic sensor can tell a rifle from, say, a milk pail, shovel, or tricycle. (U.S. Navy/MITRE)

DISCRIMINATOR. Official artist's conception of the military's new automatic electronic classification system in which the sensors themselves report on what—heavy tanks, foot traffic, and so forth—is passing by. As this and other new systems demonstrate, more and more questions of judgment and identification will be given to machines in the future. (U.S. Navy/MITRE)

SHOOTING GALLERY. Not all the firepower that can be ordered in by sensors comes from aircraft. Here is a rendering of an attack from the ground on a truck convoy being managed from the mobile station in the foreground. (U.S. Navy/MITRE)

REMOTE CONTROL KILL. Two special devices created for the European incarnation of the electronic battlefield. Above is the Covert Observation Device (COD) that takes TV pictures of one's enemies, which are transmitted back to a receiver station where the operator may want to take a Polaroid snapshot to use for further analysis. Below is the Remote Firing Device (RFD) that is intended for use with COD. It is made up of a command monitoring unit and a mine firing unit. Large amounts of munitions, such as antipersonnel mines, can be placed and then selectively detonated from the remote safety of the monitoring station. (U.S. Navy/MITRE)

PORTABLE WAR. Outside and inside views of a mobile Tactical Air Control Center from which sensor derived targets are ordered to be attacked. This particular facility was set up for the Mystic Mission exhibit of 1972 at which time the electronic battlefield was presented to America's European allies. (U.S. Navy/MITRE)

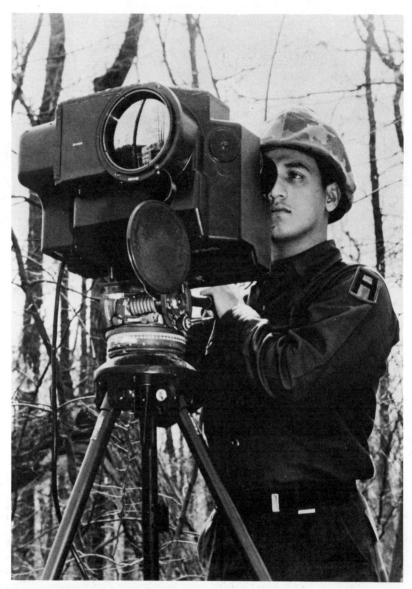

NIGHT SIGHT. One of the many night observation devices ushered into being during the Vietnam War. This particular scope is an infrared device that forms a TV-like image from the thermal radiation given off by the objects in view. (U.S. Army)

ROLLING BACK THE NIGHT. An image created by one of the new low-light level TV systems at night. (Westinghouse)

HOME FRONT. Increasingly, the electronic battlefield technology of Southeast Asia is finding application at home with some of those applications posing direct threats to privacy. The two nonthreatening examples shown here are ITT night-vision goggles now being used by the Los Angeles County Fire Department to spot fire from helicopters, and an automatic system from Sylvania that detects attempts to enter fenced-in areas. (International Telephone and Telegraph and GTE Sylvania)

CANDLEPOWER. The woman is holding a candle to have her picture taken by what is termed the world's most sensitive TV camera. The tiny GE camera, which weighs less than a pound, is one of a number of new surveillance tools with both military and civilian uses. This particular item would seem to have much potential for domestic snooping. (General Electric)

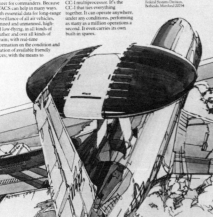

BIG BUSINESS. Advertisements from the military trade magazines show that the military is not alone in its enthusiasm for electronic battlefield hardware.

FOUR

Wiring Down the War

Inherent in the function of destroying the enemy is fixing the enemy. In the past, we have devoted sizable portions of our forces to this requirement. In the future, however, fixing the enemy will become a problem primarily in time rather than space. More specifically, if one knows continually the location of his enemy and has the capacity to mass fire instantly, he need not necessarily fix the enemy in one location with forces on the ground. On the battlefield of the future, enemy forces will be located, tracked and targeted almost instantaneously through the use of data links, computer assisted intelligence evaluation and automated fire control. With first round probabilities approaching certainty, and with surveillance devices that can continually track the enemy, the need for large forces will be less important.

> —*From an address by General William C. Westmoreland, Chief of Staff US Army, on October 14, 1969, to the Association of the US Army.*

THE GENERAL'S DREAM

The terms automated, instrumented, and electronic battlefield had been used before, but were never publicly and officially presented as a military goal as they were in the 1969 Westmoreland speech. One can dip into most any part of the speech and find the violent and hardware-heavy violent equivalent of Martin

Luther King's nonviolent "I Have a Dream" speech. "I see battlefields or combat areas," he says at one point, "that are under 24-hour real or near-real-time surveillance of all types. I see battlefields on which we can destroy anything we can locate through instant communications and the almost instantaneous application of highly lethal firepower." *

Here for the first time in an open forum both the electronic marvels of a definitely unmarvelous war and other more advanced ideas then on the drawing boards or in the minds of think tank planners were fashioned into a new philosophy of war, a manless, foolproof, giant, lethal pinball machine out of which no living thing could presumably escape. It was the advanced and totally integrated version of all those individual achievements—laser-guided bombs, remotely piloted "robot" aircraft, night-vision devices, tactical computers, the all-important sensors and more—wired into a great maze of circuits and weapons. The general assured his audience that the dream was neither far-fetched nor far-distant when he concluded in part with the line, "With cooperative effort, no more than 10 years should separate us from the automated battlefield."

And if the Westmoreland speech served to give the electronic battlefield formal expression as a new military dream, the three-day, officially secret National Security Industrial Association (NSIA) symposium on the same concept showed it was becoming the contractor's dream as well. Some 850 industry representatives with secret clearances were seated for the meeting at the National Bureau of Standards in Gaithersburg, Maryland. Meanwhile, an additional 1,450 were turned away due to the lack of space. Lest anyone think that Westmoreland and the Army were the only ones dreaming this dream, the meeting was

---

* Because of its seminal importance as a statement of military Utopia and its peculiar visionary tone—both of which are best appreciated when the speech is read as a whole—the full text is contained in Appendix A to this book.

sponsored by the Army, Navy, Air Force, Marines, and three specialized branches of the Department of Defense (including DCPG) as well as the NSIA, a military trade association.

There were other signals besides the speech and the symposium, but these were enough to show that a major shift in attitude, policy, and strategy was underway and led by the military, which only months before had been variously interested, lukewarm, cool or downright hostile to the McNamara Line, but seldom enthusiastic. Briefly, what had happened was that on its way to the front, the equipment for the McNamara Line (most particularly the antipersonnel barrier) was diverted to another use that was so successful military thinking changed overnight.

The McNamara Line was supposed to have been in operation in January, 1968, and pieces of it had actually started to be put into place as early as the fall of 1967. However, in the first days of 1968 it became obvious to American intelligence that the enemy was building up strength around the Marine base in the north-western corner of South Vietnam at Khe Sanh and that a massive attack on the base was imminent. Westmoreland, then military commander in Vietnam, gave it top priority and decided that the sensors and related equipment about to be installed along a line south of the DMZ be offered to the Marines. On January 18 a team from military headquarters in Saigon arrived at Khe Sanh to offer these new detectors which were accepted. Within 48 hours the first seismic and acoustic sensors were dropped along likely avenues of enemy approach by planes of the 7th Air Force. Almost immediately the sensors began indicating activity—up to 100 contacts a day—and after some initial confusion the Marines were learning where enemy troops were moving and in what direction.

Late in the afternoon of January 21 the base was hit with heavy rocket, mortar, and artillery fire with one of the first incoming rounds scoring a direct hit on the Marine ammunition dump, resulting in a spectacular explosion. At the same time a ground assault began on the village of Khe Sanh itself and Route 9, both of which fell within 24 hours, thereby surrounding the combat base—a situation that would not change for the next two months.

While artillery fire continued against the base, it was not until February 5 at 4:45 AM that enemy troops began attacking the entire base. It was at this time that the sensors first proved their worth by telling those inside the base what was going on outside. Though the information received from the sensors was not clearly interpreted by the still relatively inexperienced interpreters and part of it was not used at all (two enemy units clearly signalled by the sensors were somehow forgotten by one of the officers in charge of the sensors); they did forewarn of the attacking elements and prepared the Marines for later attacks on the base, which were conducted in a similar manner.

Throughout the 77-day siege the sensors came into play again and again. The official accounting of the defense of Khe Sanh contains such incidents as this one in early March, which was later described by Colonel David Lownds, commander of the 26th Marine Regiment:

The sensors which had been emplaced along Route 9 to the Laotian border suddenly came to life and it became obvious that a large column was moving adjacent to Route 9 toward the base. A personal, previous reconnaissance prior to the start of the battle gave me the time it took to reach given points along the road and the sensors were verifying the information that the NVA were proceeding as estimated. By computing the length of the column by information produced by the sensors, it became obvious to me that an enemy regiment was trying to close the base. This information coupled with possible assembly areas, allowed us to bring down upon this unit devastating firepower (*i.e.* B-52, tactical air, and artillery) to break up the impending attack. Approximately only one company was able to close and they were destroyed in front of ARVN positions on the southeast corner of the perimeter.

Clearly this kind of sensor-directed attack from the air was not uncommon. As the Regiment's intelligence officer at the time of the siege, Major Jerry E. Hudson, recalled:

During the height of activity at Khe Sanh we received several hundred air strikes, over 500 artillery missions, as many as 80 radar directed bomb missions and as high as 16 B-52 missions all in a 24-hour period. Sensors provided a prime source in the identification of targets for these systems. One B-52 mission was followed by over two hours of secondary explosions.

In April when the siege was finally lifted, the sensors came in a close second to the men themselves as objects for praise.* Regiment and base commander Lownds later estimated that without the sensors his casualties "would have almost doubled." As such reports circulated, other commanders became very enthusiastic very quickly. Among the most enthusiastic, of course, was the formerly cool Westmoreland who was soon beginning to plump for a full automated battlefield.

Khe Sanh effectively killed the McNamara Line because it showed that the new electronic equipment coming out of the

---

* One of the most fearful moments of the war came in early February during the siege when a number of rumors concerning the use of nuclear weapons began. It all began when an anonymous caller pointedly asked Senate Armed Services Committee staff director Carl Marcy why the Pentagon had sent Dr. Richard L. Garwin, a tactical nuclear expert, and three other weapons experts to Vietnam. That, added to a statement attributed to Joint Chiefs of Staff Chairman Wheeler to the effect that "all possibilities" had to be considered in the defense of Khe Sanh, made for some genuinely petrifying reports about nuclear weapons including one by presidential candidate Senator Eugene J. McCarthy that "there have been some demands already" for the use of nuclear weapons in Vietnam. Both the White House and Department of Defense vigorously denied that such weapons were under consideration or that the four experts were over there looking into their use. Actually, the four men were all either part of the DCPG staff or, like Garwin, on its Scientific Advisory Committee, and had gone over to see the antivehicular portion, which had just gone into operation under the code name Igloo White. As David Israel, one of the four on the trip, recalls, "Part of the confusion came because we couldn't say exactly why we were over there. Igloo White was very secret and very sensitive at that point and it couldn't be talked about."

DCPG effort could be used to the greatest advantage in support of ground combat operations wherever they were. There was little objection to the change in plans because decision makers all the way up the line knew that they worked in 360-degree operations like Khe Sanh but could not be sure about linear applications. Unit commanders who had heard about Khe Sanh wanted strings of sensors for their own operations whether they were defending a heliport from Viet Cong sappers, running a fire base, trying to stem waterborne infiltration in the Delta or even helping to prevent infiltration along certain routes through the DMZ.

"BETTER KILLING THROUGH ELECTRONICS" *

After Khe Sanh, sensors became so much a part of ground combat operations in Southeast Asia that the troops who learned how to work with them were soon talking about them in terms of personality quirks and characteristics, almost as if they were comrades. A former DCPG staff engineer with field experience recalls, "Some were very 'nervous' and would react to the slightest noise while others were what the boys called 'cool' in that they wouldn't react until they picked up something really worth worrying about. Certain sensors worked best with certain men who were in tune with them."

There are many, many incidents in which these sensors and their human partners played a key role, but for the Army at least the "best case" example most commonly cited occurred between June 5 and 8, 1969, at Fire Support Base Crook in Tay Ninh province near the Cambodian border.

From the early days of heavy American involvement through

* This slogan was found on a small sign pasted up in the naval operations center in a small base 20 miles west of Saigon. It was observed by Ralph Blumenthal who reported on it in a *New York Times* article of February 18, 1970.

1967, fire support bases were established as secure oases in combat zones where there were no well-defined battle lines. Initially, these American institutions—replete with medical facilities, supply depots, and artillery—were ambitious and large affairs commonly requiring three rifle companies to defend them. However, these bases of support were routinely attacked by the Viet Cong and North Vietnamese who apparently found them irresistible. In light of these constant attacks the United States began rethinking the matter, which led to a new role for the fire base. Henceforth, such bases would be set up for the specific purpose of drawing the enemy, that is, decoying him into a position where he could easily be attacked. Of course, sophisticated target detection devices were needed to find and locate the decoyed. As we already know, such instruments were on their way to the front in the form of sensors, infrared, and other night-sighting devices and new ultrasophisticated radars.

In April, 1969, the Army established Fire Base Crook to the northwest of Tay Ninh city as one of the new generation of bases. The spot picked was in the midst of a heavily used route for infiltrating men and supplies out of Cambodia and into Vietnam. "The plan," writes Lieutenant General John H. Hay, Jr., in the Army's official *Vietnam Studies: Tactical and Materiel Innovations*, "assumed that the enemy would not be able to resist an attempt to knock out the isolated post." In fact, much was done to make doubly sure an attack would be forthcoming. One ploy was deliberately leaving patches of cover around the base to attract reconnaissance parties.

At the base was a small force of the 25th Infantry Division, a few support people, and six 105-mm. howitzers. Should the bait be taken, artillery from other locations and air support were programmed to spring into action. All of this, of course, was complemented by the fullest array of detection and warning devices.

Nothing much happened for some weeks, but then at 8:00 on

the evening of June 5 the seismic sensors around the base began to pick up activity: men moving heavy equipment. The base commander, Major Joseph E. Hacia, ordered harassing fire to begin against likely assembly areas. Through the evening seismic indications of enemy activity continued and soon the base was at full alert. Then beginning about 1:30 A.M. all enemy activity seemed to cease, but the quiet did not last and at precisely 2:55 A.M. rockets, rifle fire, propelled grenades, and mortar fire began from the south and east. Damage to the base was light because most of the fire was high, but one GI manning a listening post on the perimeter was killed by a mortar round. Meanwhile, a batallion-sized ground attack was underway from the south and east.

In response, artillery fire from Crook began to saturate the area around the base while the riflemen worked to make sure that no enemy foot soldiers got too close. By 4:00 A.M. the air was filled with American tactical aircraft and gunships, which began hammering away at the enemy's rocket, mortar, and antiaircraft positions.

The heavy fire and the approach of dawn caused the enemy to withdraw, and by 5:30 A.M. the base was receiving only a little light fire. At dawn a partial sweep of the battle area by Americans revealed that the score in dead was now 76 to 1, in favor of Fire Base Crook.

The first evening's sequence of events was repeated almost exactly the second night complete with early sensor detection and harassing fire by the Americans, a suddenly quiet period about 1:00 A.M., a 2:55 A.M. attack followed quickly by an American attack and a 5:30 A.M. withdrawal. The major difference between the two night's activities was the intensity of fighting. For the Americans, only three men were wounded and damage to the base itself was minor; however, the picture was different for the other side. This picture was painted most graphically by the Army's Major General Ellis W. Williamson, who, in testifying to the efficacy of sensors at the 1970 senate hearings, used a map of the area with numbers superimposed over certain areas:

Our search of the battlefield proved just how punishing our efforts had been. At daylight additional infantry elements were flown into the battle area to assist in the sweep. Before helicopters could land on the helipad at Crook, 38 enemy bodies had to be removed. This diagram indicates where the bodies were found, and gives us an idea as to which weapons eliminated the enemy. The 60—29 plus 31—west of the river were killed almost exclusively by helicopters, the 32 along the woodline were killed by indirect artillery, and the 20 close in were killed by direct fire—rifle and machine gun—from the base, the 43 along the road were killed by the Night Hawk helicopters and the remainder of over 150 were killed by a combination of US Air Force planes and fire from within the base.

In all, on the second night, 323 additional enemy were killed and 10 prisoners taken. I had to move two bulldozers up to the area, just to bury the dead.

On the third night the base only experienced light, small arms and mortar fire causing no US casualties but produced three Viet Cong dead. There was no ground attack that night and Army historian Lieutenant General John Hay, for one, has adjudged the few shots fired as more a "parting gesture" from the decimated 272nd Viet Cong Regiment than an actual assault. "A total disaster for the enemy," is how Hay summed it up in his book, while General Williamson chose to cap his recounting of the incident for the Senate with the stark bottom line body count: 412 to 1.

While the Crook example is most often cited by those illustrating the awesome reality of the electronic battlefield in early action, it is hardly the only case with such lopsided results, or even the only case with lopsided results relative to a fire control base. At Fire Base Mahone near Dau Tieng just south of the Michelin rubber plantation one night a set of sensors indicated people were hiding in a bamboo thicket a few hundred yards away. There was no other clue to indicate enemy activity, but it was decided to open fire on the thicket with guns and mortars nonetheless. When there was no return fire and absolutely no movement in the area it was feared that there had been a false alarm; however, a daylight patrol found 21 enemy dead, four wounded, and assorted weapons including three rocket-propelled grenade launchers, a complete mortar, and a flame thrower.

Later still in the war, a third fire base concept came into being: essentially larger areas used to monitor and "interdict" troops passing through an area rather than just to draw units into fights, which the previous generation of bases had done. Fire Support Surveillance Base Floyd was one of these and covered the entire floor of a valley in northern Binh Dinh province. Basically what had been done by the 173rd Airborne Brigade, which had pioneered the new concept with Floyd, was to turn a whole area into a large electronic and explosive trap, which still happened to carry the misleading name of fire support base.

The first full-fledged display of this concept began at Fire Base Floyd before dawn on August 29, 1970, when the 3rd Battalion, 2nd North Vietnamese Army Regiment entered the valley activating the southern-most sensor for a full 20 minutes. The duration of the signal indicated a long column of men, which was confirmed by a PPS-5 radar unit. The base's tactical operations center decided to attack the rear of the column so that there would be a good chance of getting its head later as the North Vietnamese were driven deeper and deeper into the "fire base." The end of the column was hit with mortar fire while the rest of the column kept moving north as hoped. Then, to quote directly from the account of the incident in Hay's *Tactical and Materiel Innovations*:

The radar continued to track the enemy, and additional sensors became active. By this time night observation devices had picked up enemy activity. When the head of the column activated a sensor, it was hit by fire from 105-mm. howitzers, 4.2-inch mortars, and 81-mm. mortars. After this barrage, the PPS-5 and night observation devices confirmed that the enemy was fleeing to the west. Quad .50-caliber machine gun fire pursued the retreating enemy, and mortar fire blocked his escape to the west. Contact was not lost until the enemy left the killing zone.

First light revealed fewer actual bodies and body parts strewn about than had been found after the Crook and Mahone incidents, but there was still plenty of evidence to support Hay's use of the term "killing zone." One more passage from his account makes the point:

Blood trails leading west into the high ground confirmed the accuracy of the barrages. The enemy had not been able to remove all of his dead and wounded. Reconnaissance forces found six dead enemy soldiers and one wounded, along with one AK-50, one 60-mm. mortar, and numerous pieces of individual equipment that had been discarded. On 3 September a wounded enemy soldier, captured in the mountains near the 506 Valley, confirmed that the toll of dead and wounded had been great.

In addition to these varied fire base incidents, there were many other events and applications that made many Army men into true believers. Units plagued by mines planted sensors in the areas or along the roads where the problem was most severe and then shelled when activity was indicated, which either stopped or severely curtailed the mining. There were a number of reports of dead enemy soldiers who had been killed while planting the mines. Then, a number of commanders reported that sensors had enabled them to forestall rocket attacks and sapper raids on airports, cities, and so forth. The glowing United States Army reports extended to the South Vietnamese Army, which was getting sensors from the United States on a selected basis by 1970. In March 1970, the men of the 54th ARVN Regiment located at

Fire Base Anzio, south of Phu Bai, used sensors in an action that allowed them to drop 75 bodies just outside their outer perimeter without allowing one of the enemy to cross the perimeter. About a week later another sensor-equipped ARVN unit at Fire Base Nancy, north of Hue, came within 30 corpses of duplicating the Anzio feat.

Of course, sensors in themselves do not make an electronic battlefield, and it must be remembered that they were operating in tandem with other more lethal pieces of Army equipment. One item that was used almost exclusively to react to sensor readings was the Night Hawk helicopter. It carried a searchlight (both white and infrared), night observation devices, and a very rapid machine gun called the minigun.

Meanwhile, the Navy was also using sensors for its work in Vietnam although its experience with DCPG's handiwork began on a sour note.* The first aircraft configured to deliver and monitor sensors were Navy OP-2E aircraft, which were essentially cumbersome P-2s specially outfitted for sensor missions. A dozen of them were sent to Vietnam in late 1967 and three were soon lost (two to flak and one hit a mountain because of its inability to climb fast), while another four were damaged by flak. The sensor work was clearly not meant for the slow, lumbering OP-2E and by the next summer they all were replaced by faster, higher performing, Air Force planes operating at higher altitudes.

That unfortunate business aside, the Navy like the Army had been immediately impressed with what the sensors had done at Khe Sanh and quickly incorporated them in its riverine operations, specifically its SEA LORD (for Southeast Asia, Lake, Ocean, River, Delta) mission aimed a preventing waterborne infiltration. Part of the response was to create three special SEA

* Before Vietnam the Navy was already rather deeply into sensors as it had long been involved with sonobuoys as part of its antisubmarine warfare work and, in fact, the technology of the land acoubuoy borrowed much from the Navy sonobuoy.

LORD vans crammed full of monitoring equipment that could be moved by boat, helicopter, or truck. In actual Asian operations these $430,000 apiece vans were both too sophisticated and too fragile and were brought home. They were replaced by a simpler more effective read-out system.

Most Navy sensor operations were conducted against those moving on the soggy trails and shallow canals of the Delta area, which was almost impossible to effectively monitor with live troops. Infiltrators would be detected by the sensors and hit with the nearest available artillery. Here as in some other sensor operations, the Navy seldom saw those it was killing, but at least the electronics involved let them hear the attack. One such Delta episode was described by Rear Admiral William H. House in Congressional testimony:

Two airstrikes were put in an area where a Navy team had tracked a large enemy force on sensors. Acoubuoy picked up screams and yelling during the airstrike. After the first airstrike the team monitored a VC [Viet Cong] conversation in which was discussed the life of a VC, the possibility of a second airstrike, and instructions to return home. A second airstrike resulted in the enemy apparently aborting his mission.

Now, onto the Air Force and the biggest, most important example.

IGLOO WHITE

Of all the applications of the electronic battlefield, none was more sophisticated, dramatic, or lethal than Project Igloo White, which was primarily installed to cut traffic on the Ho Chi Minh Trail in Laos. As mentioned earlier, it was the highly refined, revised, and air-supported half of the original Jason proposal. It ran at full tilt from the end of 1969 until the end of 1972 at a cost of about a billion dollars per year.

The raw materials for Igloo White were tens of thousands of electronic sensors, countless tons of ordnance, scores of relay and delivery aircraft, and a gigantic, computerized nerve center, which was located in Nakhon Phanom, Thailand.

The process began with the sensors that were seeded in strings as they were flung from aircraft moving at speeds of up to 600 miles per hour to land on the roads and trails of interest. To avoid detection they were designed to be as unobtrusive as possible. Some were tree-hangers, which came down on parachutes that made them snag high in the jungle canopy where they were extremely hard to see. Others came flying out of the delivery plane and hit hard enough to bury themselves in the ground with only their antennae remaining visible. The antennae look like weeds right down to their fleshy plastic branches which moved in the breeze. When one of these disguised sensors was found and tampered with by the enemy, it would self-destruct, "Mission Impossible" style. Like most of the rest of the Igloo White system changes and improvements were made on the sensors with regularity. One major sensor development was that the unit price of sensors dropped quickly. A 1967 Acoustic Directional Seismic Intrusion Detector (ADSID) cost $2,145 but that price had dropped to $975 by 1970. This drop, added to improved batteries for longer life and greater efficiency in placing them, netted a reduction in cost-per-sensor-per-day from $100 in 1967 to less than $15 three years later.

Next came the relay aircraft that circled nearby to receive the sensor signals and pass them along to the ground center for analysis. This relay operation began with the Air Force EC-121R, a four-engine Constellation transport with a full crew, but it later gave way to the Pave Eagle, a small commercial plane (the Beech Debonair), which could operate as either a manned vehicle or an unmanned drone. Pave Eagle's advantages were that it was a very cheap, data relay platform and that it could operate unmanned in dangerous areas.

The imposing Infiltration Surveillance Center (ISC) in Thailand was the next link in the lethal chain. The ISC building itself—reputedly the largest in Southeast Asia—was the heart of the Igloo White system. Due to the large number of sensors, the information from them relayed to the Center had to first be digested and sorted by computer before it could be passed along to target analysts who, in turn, passed their assessments to the bases, which control the strike aircraft and order them to their targets. At one time during Igloo White the ISC boasted two super-sophisticated IBM 360-65 computers just to take in, sort, and store billions of bits of information. Speaking of these two computers, aerospace writer George Weiss wrote in *Military Aircraft* magazine in 1971, "In their electronic brains are the entire 3,500 miles of turning and twisting Ho Chi Minh Trail system. The locations of every crossroad, gully and sensor are known to them."

Finally there were the last members of the team: helicopter gunships, F-4s, B-52s, B-57s, and C-130s carrying the varied selection of antipersonnel and antivehicular ordnance discussed in the previous chapter. Commonly, the pilot of the F-4 Phantom or whatever would not only not see his target but not even push the button that dropped the bombs—like so much else in Igloo White this was automated with the bombs released at the moment selected by the computer. Right up until Igloo White was phased out in 1972 new munitions and delivery vehicles were tried with this element of the system. One such late entry was special AC-130 "aerial battleships" carrying the code name Pave Spectre, which as far as Southeast Asia was concerned were the last word in automated battlefield technology. This special gunship carried such sophisticated, onboard equipment as thermal sensors able to find the ignition systems of trucks. This particular trick was accomplished through a special cathode ray tube that reacts to electrical ignitions with jittery interference in much the same way that a home TV set reacts when a plane passes overhead. Here, however, the interference guided the plane to the target. Another impressive element of this flying destroyer was its 40-mm. cannon that were fired automatically in response to the onboard sensors. At the same time the plane was flown automatically in response to sensor readings to give the cannons their best shots at the targets on the ground. Shortly after they had been introduced, the Air Force claimed that one Pave Spectre aircraft had knocked out 68 trucks in one hour which, of course, is better than one a minute.

Not all of the late additions were as sophisticated as Pave Spectre. One helicopter gunship weapon was large containers of nails that were set to explode above the ground with the effect of a gargantuan sawed-off shotgun.

The normal time between target acquisition and weapons delivery in Igloo White was less than five minutes and could be in rare cases less than two minutes. At a special news briefing held at the Pentagon in February, 1971, Air Force Brigadier General William G. Evans, a two year DCPG veteran who had just been made the Air Force's Special Assistant for Sensor Exploitation, gave an example of a typical quick reaction Igloo White truck killing operation:

The sensors are delivered in strings along the roads . . . and their activations are constantly monitored by an assessment officer in the Infiltration Surveillance Center. As a truck convoy passes a string, it activates the sensors, one after the other. From the activation pattern, the computer can determine the speed of the convoy and thereby predict its time of arrival at a point further down the road designated as a strike zone. As the convoy passes through successive sensor strings, this time of arrival is updated and refined. The expected time of arrival of the convoy at point X and the coordinates of that point are passed to F-4 fighter-bombers; the pilots enter this data into the aircrafts' computers. This gives the course to steer to that point and programs an automatic release of the aircrafts' ordnance so that the bombs' time of arrival at point X will coincide with that of the trucks. There is a short sensor string, or gate, really, just short of point X to provide a last-minute confirmation of the convoy's arrival in the strike zone before the ordnance is released.

You'll notice I said strike *zone;* we are not bombing a precise point on the ground with a point target bomb—we can't determine each truck's location that accurately with ground sensors, which are listening—not viewing—devices. Since we never actually "see" the trucks as point targets, we use area-type ordnance to cover the zone we know the trucks to be in. Ground sensors have proven quite adequate to make this all-weather bombing technique effective. Thus, by marrying sensor-derived intelligence with an accurate delivery system and area munitions, we have an interdiction system which can hurt the enemy, even when he seeks the cover of foliage, weather or darkness. And the system is completely air-supported; no ground forces are needed.

Not all targets were picked so quickly, as there was another side to the sensors: an ability to detect targets that would hold ("non-time sensitive targets" in Air Force jargon) such as truck parks and storage areas. Commonly a group of trucks would pass a sensor string and noted by the man assessing the situation in the ISC. He waits for the trucks to signal their arrival at the next string but nothing happens. Several times during the night the same thing happens again and, perhaps, the same first string picks up a group of trucks heading north, which had never showed up on strings lower down the Trail. The tentative conclusion here would be that there was a truck park located between the two strings, a conclusion that would be checked by adding a new string of acoustic sensors to hear what was going on. If confirmed, an attack would be launched.

Incidentally, there is something downright otherworldly about the ability of acoustic sensors to let one eavesdrop on his prey in hi-fi. For my benefit a tape that had been made from an acoustic sensor was played by an engineer at the MITRE Corporation. It contained a few critical minutes in a North Vietnamese truck park along the Ho Chi Minh Trail in Laos and was recorded during an

Igloo White mission. The first sound heard is that of a single truck parked with its engine running. It can be heard for several minutes during which time the only other sound one can make out is distant artillery. Then a voice can be heard shouting excitedly. The first truck is now moving and others are starting and some drivers are using their horns. Suddenly, there is the unmistakable sound of a jet zeroing in, followed by a quick series of sharp explosions and the jet pulling away. Save for the sound of a few of the surviving trucks which are getting more and more distant, there is relative quiet for a few moments and then comes the sudden and loud *pockata-pockata* of antiaircraft fire.

Such vignettes—and there were many—must be considered a milestone in the history of war in that technology now permits one to listen in on an attack you are directing from a control center hundreds of miles away.* Only a TV picture is lacking.

All of this—the blind bombing by computer, listening in on those being bombed, enemies who never saw each other and more—had the ring of grim fantasy. Those who tried to report on it found themselves working with images, metaphors, and compar-

---

* There is a rich collection of stories about what was heard during the war with acoustic sensors. Many are certainly apocryphal—such as the accounts of seduction of North Vietnamese WACS within sensor range—but one that is not was contained on a tape played before a senate committee. A member asked if the sensors were ever discovered and in answer a tape was played in which a sensor snagged in a tree was spotted. Then came the sound of axes as the soldiers chopped away at the tree and, finally, a crash and screaming. Asked what had happened, the Air Force officer who had brought the tape replied, "Sir, the tree must have fallen on them."

Another nonapocryphal sensor anecdote was related to me by former DCPG Deputy Director Dave Israel who says that the first enemy encounter with an acoustic sensor came when two communist soldiers spotted one snagging in a tree. He says, "A tape was made of their reaction to it and it was rushed back to Washington where we got the CIA to translate it for us. We were very eager to find out how the enemy would react to it and how much he understood about what we were doing. It turned out to be a non-com telling one of his men to get the hell up in the tree to get the thing and the soldier telling him to go screw himself. We discovered that the man wanted it for the parachute which he would give to his girlfriend to make a dress out of."

isons previously reserved for science fiction. "Only in this war," wrote George Weiss in one of his several articles on the subject, "can you find the veterans of a hundred computer battles who have never heard a shot fired, pilots who bomb acres, not pinpoints, and fly by computers, bombs which drop on electronic signal, drones that fly without manual control—and the entire system tied to a collection of tubes, transistors and diodes that calculate time and space with the precision of an astronaut's moon landing." The opening words to a *Christian Science Monitor* article on Igloo White read, "Buck Rogers is alive and well and bombing Indochina," and when the author of this book first wrote about Igloo White for *The Washington Monthly* with coauthor John Rothchild we came up with this image for what was going on, "As it now stands, a body becomes a number only after death in Vietnam, but with the new Battlefield [read Igloo White], even a living soldier will be a numerical blip on a lighted panel, his existence or destruction known only by a blip along the sensor paths, a Tinkerbell whose death is signaled when the blip disappears from the tracking machine, meaning that the drone helicopter has arrived and gone."

But when it came to Igloo White the writer's images and metaphors were no stranger than the straightest reporting. Writer and pilot Frank Harvey went to Vietnam to report on the 1972 version of the air war for *Worldview* magazine and brought back this picture of things as they were at the ISC in Thailand as the movement of a truck convoy was being monitored:

The movement of the convoy as it prints out brightly on the radar screen at the control center is known as "the worm." Sometimes two convoys are seen converging on each other, and the controllers wait until they meet and there is a stoppage of traffic. Then they vector Air Force and/or Navy jets to the spot. So sophisticated is the delivery that the pilots simply sit there, directed by their own airborne computers, until the black boxes drop the bomb for them. The accuracy and effect of these drops is then, of course, measured back at the control headquarters by observing what the worms do. Usually they wiggle away a little—then vanish. The reason is they've been wiped out.

The results claimed for the system by the Air Force and DCPG in wiping out "worms" was fantastic: 12,000 trucks in 1971, its last full year of operation; 12,000 for 1970; 6,000 in 1969; and 5,500 in 1968, its first full year in operation. In all, over 35,000 trucks, each of which (again, according to official estimates) carried 10,000 pounds of war supplies intended for South Vietnam. Measured by another variable, the Air Force estimated in early 1971 that only 20 percent of the supplies coming down the Trail through Laos made it through. Time and again the Pentagon gave a score for Igloo White in terms of trucks and cargos destroyed, but never in terms of human death. As it can be assumed that there was at least one North Vietnamese to a truck (to say nothing of dispatchers, mechanics, and porters) and since many of the weapons were primarily antipersonnel, it would seem both reasonable and conservative to estimate that as many men as trucks were killed or wounded by Igloo White.

Besides men and trucks the physical damage to the area was great. Unfortunately, few representatives of the Western media were able to get a glimpse of the Ho Chi Minh Trail during the height of the Igloo White campaign (save for the cathode ray tube images at ISC) but one who did was an *Agence France* press correspondent who reported this scene:

On each side of the road there are heaps of scrap metal, pieces of aircraft, the containers of antipersonnel bombs, empty munitions casings, 37-mm. cannon shells, detonated antipersonnel mines . . . At certain points, it is impossible to walk on the sides of the roads. You sink up to your knees in an impalpable dust, the earth having become dust under the impact of the bombs and incendiary weapons . . .

When the monsoon comes, that dust turns to mud and slides onto the roads . . . nothing lives in this dust, not even crickets. Only man is resisting it.

Igloo White finally began shutting down in December 1972 when the military told the press that the exactly four-year old system was being phased out for two reasons: prospects for a cease fire were good and its operating costs were too high at a time when the US was limiting the costs of the war. Not stated, but understood by all, was the fact that the Air Force by late 1972 was concentrating on hitting supplies while still in North Vietnam before they got to the Trail. Moreover, while there was still certainly some traffic on the Trail it had apparently dwindled. In late October, Malcolm W. Browne of *The New York Times* reported from Nakhon Phanom, Thailand, "The infiltration of North Vietnamese troops and war materiel through Laos and Cambodia into the western flank of South Vietnam appears to have dropped almost to the vanishing point, according to American pilots at this base adjoining the Ho Chi Minh Trail."

Officially, Igloo White was a great success. *Air Force* magazine termed it ". . . a long stride forward in our search for a more effective deterrent to conventional war." Others, like Air Force chief sensorman General Evans, talked about the vast and untapped potential for exploiting the technology of Igloo White in the future. A few chose more colorful words of praise. "We wired the Ho Chi Minh Trail like a drugstore pinball machine and we plug it in every night," said an Air Force officer to a reporter from *Armed Forces Journal*, adding, "Before, the enemy had two things going for him. The sun went down every night and he had trees to hide under. Now he has nothing."

One problem demonstrated by the electronic battlefield in Southeast Asia is that when fighting and killing is remote, it allows those in control of the system to control information about it. With Igloo White, for instance, the public, the press, and Congress were forced to rely on the computer printout of results based on the Air Force's method of scoring. This allowed the military to reveal just that information it wished to have consumed. Igloo White scoring procedures did not account for, as just pointed out, enemy deaths nor for the American pilots and crewmen who died from the antiaircraft fire and SAMs from the Trail—about all that was ever publicly announced was that the United States was "taking losses" as part of the Igloo White operation.* Another matter was civilians. "The Trail does not run through entirely deserted landscapes . . ." said a special study group at Cornell University in its 1971 study, *The Air War in Indochina*, which went on to say that at least 13,000 refugees were created around the Trail through 1970, and that the population of the provinces through which the Trail ran was 250,000. Figures on civilian injury and death were unavailable as the government was keeping them secret.

Despite strong evidence to the contrary, one has only to read through a few of the official briefings and descriptions that were given of Igloo White to see that the image being pushed is that of a clean, efficient machine functioning like a large, electronic chess set. Such nasty considerations as pain, civilian casualties, blood, and death (foreign or American) were deleted. Also, one finds that the official versions of Igloo White, the Fire Base Crook incident, and other examples of the electronic battlefield in action were written without direct reference to malfunction, improper targeting, breakdown, or anything else negative.

There were, however, others who raised some points about all of this. One very questionable aspect of the electronic battlefield, especially Igloo White, was the glowing statistics issued to show

* Available clues indicate that American losses were far from light. For one thing, it is known that during the life of Igloo White more and more defensive installations were added by those on the Trail. It is also known that a minimum of 600 planes and helicopters were lost during the air war in Laos, and it is not unreasonable to assume that a half to two-thirds were part of Igloo White.

how well it was working. Although they attracted little attention at the time, the most important comments on the Igloo White box score were released in a report from the Senate Committee on Foreign Relations' Subcommittee on United States Security and Commitments Abroad entitled "Laos: April, 1971," which was based on a fact-finding mission to Laos by members of the Committee staff. It said, in part:

> The reported figures for the number of North Vietnamese and Pathet Lao trucks damaged or destroyed on the Trail are growing at a geometric rate . . . These figures are not taken seriously by most US officials, even Air Force officers, who generally apply something on the order of a 30% discount factor. One reason why there is some skepticism about the truck kills claimed by the Air Force is the total figure for the last year greatly exceeds the number of trucks believed by the Embassy to be in all of North Vietnam.

The report went on to explain that when a shell hit within 10 feet of a truck, the Air Force credited itself with a "damaged," and if there was a hit of any kind it went down in the books as a "kill." One officer told the Senate investigators that he assumed the North Vietnamese were smart enough to set off decoy explosives during attacks so that they would be counted as dead or damaged even if not hurt at all. Regarding public statements on the ability of Igloo White to cut off supplies—at times the military claimed that as little as 10 percent of that which began down the Trail actually came out the other end—heavy discount factors were being applied by those in the know and those with the ability to put two and two together. Senate staff members reported widespread skepticism by United States officials on the scene about the official claims being made in Washington. Their logic was that the North Vietnamese continued to be able to get those goods into South Vietnam and Cambodia that were needed to support their operations. That line of reasoning got an added boost just before

Igloo White was shut down in 1972 because of that year's communist tank and artillery offensive in certain parts of South Vietnam including the An Loc region north of Saigon. Presumably, scores of tanks and artillery pieces moved down the Trail right by the ears of Igloo White.

Then, there is the matter of performance itself. To this day most former DCPG staffers and others who worked with the system are loath to talk about situations in which their creation malfunctioned or did not perform at its intended high levels. Typically, they talk like this former DCPG engineer who told me, "I know that in all those instances I heard about in which the sensors supposedly didn't work we learned that they were actually misapplied or used improperly. Usually what we'd find had happened when someone said a sensor wasn't working was that it had been incorrectly emplaced. For example, we'd find acoustic sensors with antennae that had somehow gotten buried."

Significantly, however, one high placed member of the DCPG inner circle who now admits that things were not exactly as portrayed to the press, public, and Congress is David R. Israel, who was DCPG Deputy Director and in that capacity was awarded the Secretary of Defense Meritorious Civilian Service Medal (the highest civilian award made by the Pentagon). When I talked with him in June 1975, he was working for the Federal Aviation Agency as acting associate director for engineering. "It was a success in many ways," he said. "Technically, the sensors worked well although there were some out and out failures like an early infrared sensor that we could never get to work right and had to be dropped.* DCPG was in itself an effective *tour de force* in that it showed how much could be done by a group of top people working without restrictions in a short period of time. But there were operational problems. We had no trouble finding

---

* This would be the insect-attracting PIRID mentioned earlier.

targets with our sensors but destroying them successfully from the air was another. A lot got through." I asked him if this was the real reason why Igloo White came to an end when it did—essentially because too much money was being spent at that point on too few destroyed trucks? "More or less," he replied.

There have also been a few people who have actively criticized the performance of the new technology. One such man was J.J. Brown, a former Air Force captain who was a photo intelligence officer in Southeast Asia from 1966 through 1968, who made his charges in a two-part newspaper feature for Dispatch News Service International carrying a Singapore dateline in June, 1972. Brown's contention was that some of the electronic gadgetry is "defective and unworkable," and that the military was making unsupportable claims for many of its new toys. "Had the sensor network been effective," he said of Igloo White, "the communists would not have been able to defeat Saigon troops at Tchepone in 1971 or move tanks and armored vehicles into South Vietnam as they have recently." His sharpest criticism was saved for the RF4C reconnaissance jet that worked as part of the overall system. The plane contained three sensing systems—normal camera, infrared camera, and side-looking radar—none of which, he wrote, did their job properly. His points regarding the plane were quite specific, for instance: "The infrared in the RF4C is called the RS7. It is of no value unless the aircraft is below 2,000 feet. At night this altitude is very dangerous and almost impossible to maintain."

One of the most often heard stories about the electronic battlefield had to with the chemical sensor or so-called "people sniffer." The gist of the story was that the North Vietnamese and Viet Cong would hang bags or buckets of urine in trees to trigger the sensors and get the Americans to waste their munitions firing into the trees. Save for this trick—not employed quite as often as the number of times the story has been told and variously embellished would indicate—sensor spoofing was not a big problem.* It could have been, it seems. Pierre Boulle, author of *Planet of the Apes* and *Bridge Over the River Kwai*, in the first novel about sensor war, *Ears of the Jungle*, describes an ingenious team of North Vietnamese agents with a Chinese advisor who trick the sensors on a massive scale. Among other twists, he has them playing recordings of crickets to mask the sounds of real trucks and playing recordings of trucks to have the Americans waste their bombs and in the process perform tasks like killing wild buffalo to feed the troops and clearing areas for future roads. In a great spoof on Igloo White, Boulle actually sets up a complex plan in which the sensors and the bombers involved (with their automated ordnance delivery) get tricked into bombing the ISC in Thailand thereby reducing its computers to so much rubble.

"These were fascinating ideas," says Israel, "and quite imaginative but things never quite worked out like Boulle predicted. They never really tried to spoof them on any scale. Sure they shot some, burned others and in what was perhaps the ultimate act of contempt we actually heard them piss on one of our acoustic sensors; but they never really played games with us." This has kept the sensor crowd guessing ever since. "The only logical conclusions you can come to are that either the enemy didn't understand what they were and how much damage they were doing or that they weren't hurting the enemy as much as we thought they were and decided to let them be," says Lieutenant-Colonel R. R. Darron, USMC, a man with extensive sensor experience. Darron and others find it hard to buy either conclusion.

Much harsher than spoofing, however, is the charge that was

* Tales of the trick have left some with the impression that chemical sniffers were a joke. Not so. In August 1968 for instance, the 1st Brigade of the Army's Ninth Division reported using the sniffer to pinpoint two enemy companies from which 104 soldiers were killed.

leveled by Colonel David H. Hackworth, one of the military's most highly decorated officers who retired from the service at the end of the Vietnam war because of his disagreement with the way the war had been fought. In an article he wrote entitled "Our Great Vietnam Goof!", which appeared in the June 1972 *Popular Mechanics*, he maintained that the biggest error of the war was the gadgets, exotic new weapons, and unreliable versions of basic weapons that Americans were sent to fight with. His list of specifics is long—uniforms ill-suited for the jungle, inflatable shelters begging to be deflated by a VC sniper, a standard issue radio handset "as delicate as a fine piece of porcelain," and so forth—and includes specific reference to an incident in March 1971 when Viet Cong sappers overran an Americal Division fire base killing 33 and wounding 76. The base was supposedly protected by sensors and ground radar, which prompted Hackworth to comment, "If an unsophisticated enemy like the Vietcong can breach defenses protected by the latest that science and technology can offer, it stands to reason that a more sophisticated enemy can easily overcome any electronic battlefield it may encounter in the future."

But for every critical military leader like Hackworth, there seem to be a dozen or so willing to go out of their way to pay homage to the new technology of beep and bang. Opening with the seminally important and cybernetically visionary Westmoreland statement of October 1969, strong testimonial has continued to pour from seemingly every military quarter down to and including such normally dry and unemotional places as combat manuals and technical reports. A 1973 Army manual, *Unattended Ground Sensing Devices*, produced by the Combat Surveillance and Electronic Warfare School at Fort Huachuca, Arizona, says, "Considering the many UGS-related [Unattended Ground Sensors] innovations and applications being explored, the UGS program is expected to become the most revolutionary advancement for conducting successful combat operations since the introduction of the radio many years ago." At another point the same manual says that the uses of sensors ". . . have thus far been limited only by the imagination of the users"—a comment that sounds more like it comes from an ad from a new Procter and Gamble "washday miracle" than a how-to guide to military sensor seeding.

Rave reviews were everywhere . . . and still continue to come in. Tactical historian Hay terms the sensors and their associated equipment a "major advance," the authors of the *Pentagon Papers* used the term "momentous" to characterize the policy shift their adoption signaled, the DOD's official *Commander's Digest* devoted a whole issue to recounting electronic battlefield applications in Vietnam and telling about their future promise. Pentagon research chief John Foster termed the military sensor "one of the most important products of the military experience in Vientam" and as early as 1969 was saying publicly that sensors had already revolutionized land combat. The cheers seemed to be loudest in front of the Congressional witness table where military officers were seemingly trying to outdo each other in finding new ways to praise their new infant. In the Senate electronic battlefield hearings about to be discussed in more detail, these claims, among others, were made: that a sensor-equipped battalion could keep twice the area under effective surveillance that a non-sensor battalion could, and that they had materially contributed to the lessening of the death ratio in Vietnam from 12 American deaths per 100 dead enemy to three per 100.

Even when one attempts to drag forth a negative aspect or side effect of the electronic battlefield from a military man, the reply usually comes out sounding more like a compliment. A colonel directly associated with advanced sensor applications for the Advanced Research Projects Agency paused for a moment when asked for the dark side of sensor warfare and said, "Some commanders in Southeast Asia were critical because the sensors gave them more targets to deal with at a time when they already had enough targets which had been discovered without sensors." In other words, they were *too* efficient.

This overwhelmingly positive reaction to the electronic battlefield was understandable for each of the services and the Department of Defense knew that even if there were some imperfections in the early Southeast Asian version of the system, its value had been proven and the next step was to develop bigger, better, and more efficient components for the apparatus that Westmoreland had outlined. Vietnam has been the field laboratory for the idea and for the most part it worked. Not only were better versions of the devices used in Southeast Asia needed, but so were new items and other electronic innovations that had been developing independently but which easily fit into the overall concept of an automated war machine. All that was needed now was a green light from those who authorize payment of the bills.

FIVE

A Conquered Congress

I think this constitutes probably the greatest step forward in warfare since gunpowder.

—Senator Barry Goldwater
on the electronic
battlefield, July 14, 1970.

SENATE MANO A MANO

By 1970 it had become clear that the traditional, human war machine was not only costly, inefficient, and difficult to draft, but seemingly tearing itself apart. This was the year when "fragging" became a grisly addition to the national vocabulary, that the true extent of the drug addiction epidemic (not to mention plain, old drug use) became known, that TV cameras were recording the voices and faces of soldiers refusing to obey their officers in combat areas, that the My Lai incident and coverup were still making news, and that thousands of soldiers were AWOL. The military draft was being dismantled with the full knowledge of those in power that it would probably never work again, especially for a protracted military adventure abroad. It was also the year of President Nixon's "incursion" into Cambodia, which showed, by way of a loud and violent domestic shudder that included Kent State, that an invasion force of 25,000 men was intolerable; but

100

that the American bombing attacks on Cambodia that went on before and after the invasion were somehow easier to swallow.

So it was not without good reason that the appeal of a new technological form of war that was far less dependent on men should be great at this moment in history. Yet, even at this time, it was still surprising that Congress would so easily give such a broad stamp of approval (apparently without an expiration date) to a concept that is still consuming billions from the Treasury, which will dictate the tactical response of the United States in future wars, and which continues to raise unanswered moral, tactical, and technical questions. Here then is the odd story of how America gave the OK on one of the most important new weapons systems in history almost without question or publicly expressed second thoughts.

Except for certain general bits of information on sensor technology and terse reports on the progress of the McNamara Line that was presented to the military committees by the military, up through 1970 Congress was almost totally in the dark regarding both the overall concept of the automated battlefield and its specific applications in Vietnam. Even key members had only the sketchiest details. Senator Stuart Symington, a member of the Senate Armed Services Committee and former secretary of the Air Force, let it be known that he was not aware of the initial electronic line plan until he read about it in *Newsweek* in 1967. As he retold the story later, "I thereupon went to the chairman of the committee [Senator John Stennis] and asked whether he knew about it. Before that, I went to the staff and asked whether it had ever come before the Armed Services Committee. I was told no by both, no, that it had never come before the committee, despite the hundreds of millions of dollars involved, which later turned into billions." Symington and one other Armed Services Committee member pushed for and got a briefing on the system, but later in a meeting of the Defense Subcommittee of the Senate Appropriations Committee, Symington and two other senators were denied any information on the system by military witnesses who declared it too sensitive even for presentation in executive (closed and secret) sessions.

This situation continued to be true for about three years beyond the time the early elements of the system were established facts. Nothing happened, in fact, until months after the Westmoreland "dream" speech of October 1969, after the Washington conference for 850 potential contractors, and after *Business Week* had excitedly estimated that the automated battlefield had already cost over $2 billion and would total up to $20 billion by 1980.

Finally on July 6, 1970, Congressional inattention was interrupted when Senator William Proxmire said, "Mr. President, I rise today to point out a classic example of the Pentagon's 'foot in the door technique,' one of the main reasons why the military budget is out of control. I am informed that the Pentagon has already spent some $2 billion on a secret weapons system called the electronic battlefield . . . To my knowledge this weapons system, as a weapons system, has never been authorized in the annual procurement bill in which major weapons systems are examined, judged and passed on by the House and Senate."

From this opening, Proxmire went on to detail a half-dozen problems and questions that bothered him about this battlefield project, which, as he put it, "I think it is safe to say that most Congressmen have never heard of." His pointed and diverse concerns were these:

Congressional control—Simply stated, the Senator was angry that information on this program had been kept from Congress and its costs hidden within the Defense Department budget request. "How," he asked, "is Congress to control expenditures if it does not even have knowledge, much less control, over major programs such as the electronic battlefield?"

Policy—Quoting Westmoreland to the effect that a "quiet revolution in ground warfare" was going on in Vietnam, Proxmire said that there was a whole series of questions about this process by which the military through the secret development of weapons could, because of the nature of those weapons, affect America's future military and foreign policy. These had to be answered.

Money—Three major questions: Is it worth it? How much will it ultimately cost? Will Congress be confronted with a "decision" over the automated battlefield over which it actually has little financial control because of the lengths to which it has already been carried?

Reliability—Ever concerned with overruns, malfunctioning systems, and high replacement costs, Proxmire was bothered by what he alleged to be the "extreme vulnerability" of the equipment and feared it might break down under rough handling. He had already heard of one infrared night observation device for use over medium range distances that had been abandoned because it was unable to withstand combat conditions.

Indiscriminate killing—To repeat Proxmire exactly on a most important issue raised most clearly: "One of the biggest problems is that it may be an indiscriminate weapon. The sensors cannot tell the difference between soldiers and women and children. It has been pointed out that in such underdeveloped parts of the world as Vietnam, whole villages may be wiped out by seeding wide areas with air dropped explosive devices designed to kill anyone who ventures into their neighborhood. Once seeded, we would lose control over these devices and they could represent a permanent menace to the civilian population, much like old land mines."

As a finale to this initial Congressional airing of the subject, Proxmire read a letter he had written to Secretary of Defense Melvin Laird that asked a number of specific questions about the automated battlefield including those just outlined.

Proxmire's presentation, which took about ten minutes to deliver, was not lost in the welter of the day's business because

Proxmire distributed advance copies of his remarks to the press. The Associated Press and a number of papers including both the *New York Times* and *Washington Post* printed the story.

Meanwhile, the statement and the publicity it generated was not sitting well with Senator Barry Goldwater who during the next day's session made this comment while speaking in behalf of legislation that would abolish the draft, "One of the reasons, I think, that we can go to a volunteer force, is that the Army, which is the great user of men, is depending on what our friend from Wisconsin discussed as the 'electronic battlefield' yesterday." He then added, "He did it in a very critical way, and I might say it is so highly classified that even the Armed Services Committee has not been able to hold hearings on it; but as long as he has sprung it, so to speak, I can mention it."

In light of the normally polite folkways and deferential language of the Senate, what Goldwater had done was to publicly chide the Senator from Wisconsin in strong terms. *The Washington Daily News* termed the Goldwater response a display of "Senatorial wrath." Proxmire, in turn, responded slowly but in the strongest terms when he rose again the following Monday, a week after the initial statement and six days after the Goldwater remark, to lash back. "The clear inference from the statement of the Senator from Arizona," he said for openers, "is that I have made public or released what was previously secret or classified information . . . I think there is no other inference that can be made from that statement . . . But I am here to say now that the statement was wrong and the Senator from Arizona was wrong. I did not 'spring' any classified or secret information. I did not 'lower the wall of secrecy' surrounding the electronic battlefield."

After explaining that as a matter of principle he never accepted classified information of any kind, he dropped what in terms of the Senate norm was a bombshell, to wit: "I think that both the statement which the Senator from Arizona made on the floor of the Senate, and the inferences which can not only be drawn from it but which have been drawn from it, are so serious that I have notified him of the speech I am giving now and I will ask him when I finish my speech today to make a public withdrawal of his statement and to deny the inference which has been drawn from it."

Next, Proxmire moved on to detail his sources—all unclassified—and in the process to drop his second bombshell. He pointed out that while he and his staff had gathered much valuable information from such sources as the aforementioned *Business Week* article, another in *Product Engineering,* an expensive but unclassified report from McGraw-Hill's DMS Market Intelligence Reports and two articles by United States Army generals (in *Army* magazine and *Defense Industry Bulletin*), his "gold mine" had been the Westmoreland speech of the previous October. That speech, he added, had not only been introduced into *The Congressional Record* at the time but had been inserted there by none other than Senator Goldwater under the heading of "New Developments in Ground Warfare." As is so common in Congress, Goldwater was using the *Record* as a repository for whatever happened to strike his fancy and this particular entry, like so many thousands of other items that get tossed into the hopper each session, had apparently been printed and promptly forgotten.*

"But in fairness to the Senator from Arizona," said Proxmire puckishly, "I do not charge and urge no one else to charge, that he has improperly revealed secret or classified information. That would be as unfair an inference about him as his statement was

---

* With the speech Goldwater made a few comments including this one that showed his initial enthusiasm for the system, although it leaves something to be desired in terms of clarity, "I have seen a number of these devices in action and I am very enthusiastic about what they will do for our ground forces and eventually, because the theory can be applied to all forces what we will accomplish in the field of intelligence of the economy for the entire military."

about me." And to give it all a final twist he added, "It may be that what the Senator from Arizona is really complaining about is that information originally developed for the use of the dues-paying members of the military-industrial complex has been drawn to the attention of a majority of the Members of the Senate."

The next day Goldwater, who had already sent a note of explanation to Proxmire, was quick to point out that he was not "chiding" the Senator from Wisconsin nor did he believe that any secrets had been laid bare; but he did stop short of an apology and the two men were soon again bantering about what was true and false and what was secret and unclassified. At times Goldwater clearly got carried away and made claims that immediately led to even more questions about the electronic battlefield. At one point he said that part of the system was a device that can "see through things" and which, ". . . can tell the pilot of an airplane what the fuel level is in gasoline or petroleum tanks that he is attacking." Although that claim has been steadfastly denied by the military in subsequent hearings, Goldwater planted the notion that such a piece of Superman equipment existed, which it apparently does not. If it does, however, it was Goldwater then who spilled the top secret beans.

The Senator from Arizona also took this occasion to say something about the innocence of electronic sensors, which for the previous two-and-a-half years had been wedded to an array of fearsome antipersonnel weapons to form Igloo White. Goldwater said:

This is not a weapons system. This system can kill no one. The only killing it could do is to kill itself, if the operator desires to do so. There is nothing in them that can cause casualties. It is not an electronic battlefield, although that name has been given to it by some people. It is a sensor system and that only. There is no weaponry connected with it.

This Pollyannaish portrait, of course, led to the logical question of what good was a billion dollar military system that cannot harm an enemy.

Of all the points that Goldwater made that July day, the most interesting came when he said, "The increase in sophistication of this equipment has been nothing short of fabulous. Again I am not allowed to say some of the things I have seen it do, some of the ways it is helping our men in Laos particularly—our airmen and ground forces." When Proxmire again brought up the subject more than two weeks later on July 31, he reminded Goldwater that the United States was not supposed to have troops in Laos. Goldwater later agreed and amended his earlier statement to the effect that it had aided airmen in Laos thereby helping American ground forces in South Vietnam. He then said, without any prompting, "The real guts, you might say, of our sensor system is in Thailand, where it is used on the Ho Chi Minh Trail."

While the Proxmire and Goldwater discussions were going on several important things happened. With the exception of a few determined reporters, the press attention, which had pretty much fallen away from the subject with the "demise" of the McNamara Line, was again picking up.* For example, Jack Anderson got onto the story and used his syndicated column to claim not entirely correctly that the taxpayer had already laid out $4 billion (twice the amount that Proxmire was alleging), that most of the devices used in Southeast Asia were not working and most of those that were functioning only worked for a week on the average before they conked out. Others developed other angles to the story. Ken W. Clawson, before taking his post–Watergate role as an apologist for the Nixon administration, reported in *The*

---

* The most determined followers of the scheme up to this point had been Orr Kelly of *The Washington Star* and Warren Burkett of McGraw-Hill World News. Burkett wrote both the *Business Week* and *Product Engineering* stories that helped attract Proxmire's attention in the first place.

Washington Post that Attorney General John Mitchell had told him that the same electronic sensors used in Vietnam were used along the Mexican border to detect "wetbacks and narcotics smugglers" and that they might come into play in civil disorders where they could be used to protect vital institutions. That plus a comment made by research chief John Foster to Proxmire to the effect that sensor technology would soon be made available for civilian use served to touch off a host of new questions and concerns about a domestic system with vast Big Brother implications.

Second, the rest of Congress was becoming increasingly interested in this big ticket item, which they had been kept in the dark about for so long. "Most members of the Senate I have talked to did not know we had such a program," said Proxmire who added at another point, ". . . I am willing to guess that not more than 10 or 15 Senators knew anything about it all, knew that there was any effort of any kind."

Third, the Pentagon finally got around to responding to Proxmire's questions with a statement at the end of July. Clearly, this statement which took a charge and rebuttal form was a case of too little too late. In the face of the Proxmire and Goldwater interchange, it was completely underwhelming, dry, and in places so literal as to be misleading. It made a big point that there was no official "electronic battlefield" program, which was technically true since the term had not been formally listed as such, but the fact remained that the term (along with automated and instrumented battlefield) had become the hottest of Pentagon buzzwords. Further, it tended to bring up more questions than it answered as it did with this rebuttal, quoted in its entirety, to the charge that it could not discriminate between the enemy, and women and children:

Discrimination by sensing devices is costly. However, the fundamental policy followed is that the judgement of the commander, integrating all intelligence data, is essential prior to using fire power or strike forces. Without reaction, sensors are harmless.

This was a far cry from the information that Proxmire was gathering on his own. A member of the Special Forces who had monitored sensors in Vietnam told Proxmire, "All we know is that something is moving out there. It could be the wind, an elephant or an enemy soldier. We really have almost no idea what we are shooting at." The same man was able to cite several instances where patrols had searched areas shelled in response to sensor information and found only dead water buffalos.

Clearly the renewed press interest and building Congressional interest, the Pentagon's too-literal response and more questions like the ones that had first been raised were pushing the Senate towards a full-fledged investigation. Proxmire was keeping the heat on with new questions. One pointed set that he asked in the middle of August sounded like this: "The devices which have been developed so far are largely designed for use in guerrilla warfare . . . The question must be asked, to what extent will such devices, by improving our capacity to fight such wars, encourage our involvement in future Vietnams? No one can answer with any certainty but what cannot be denied is that we will have the technology—we will have the capability, and there will be a constant temptation to make use of it. In view of this, do we want, do we need these sensor surveillance devices?" The confusion on Goldwater's part as to whether it was at work in Laos, Thailand, or both was telling in this regard as it had apparently become so easy to plug in the system that it was hard for a Senator to remember which nations the United States had electronically penetrated. Was this not the foot in the door that would inevitably lead to technicians and then foot patrols going into Laos or wherever to install, replace and evaluate equipment, especially the hand-implanted devices? Proxmire's concern with sensors as feet in the door had him using the words "more Vietnams," which in

1970, as now, had almost magical powers in awakening Congress-men. And for those that did not respond to this, there were the widely different positions on how big and expensive the system was. In explaining why the electronic battlefield was not showing up as a separate line item in the Pentagon budget and why the Senate should not worry, Armed Services Chairman Senator John Stennis said reassuringly, "This is not a large system." Meanwhile, Proxmire was finding more evidence of vast sums already spent right down to single pieces of equipment, such as a night vision gunsight for helicopters, which were costing a half-million dollars a copy.

After hours of floor debate, it had become apparent by the middle of August that Proxmire's patience was thinning and he wanted answers. When on August 17 he found that an amend-ment that he was going to attach to a military bill to force some accounting on the matter was not going to make it, he threatened to make an issue of the electronic battlefield every time military appropriations or authorization bills came to the floor. The threat clearly involved eating up a lot of Senate time in the future as he pledged to pursue the issue "in depth and at length" every time military matters were discussed.

That threat was the last straw and on August 20, 1970, Stennis announced that special hearings would take place in November to look into the "worthiness" of the electronic battlefield. On the same day, Proxmire, in his role as chairman of the Joint Economic Committee, instructed the General Accounting Office (GAO) in its capacity as Congressional investigator to answer certain questions about the system's effectiveness. In making his an-nouncement, Stennis hastily pointed out, "There's no scandal, it needs to be better understood." The remark sounded as though these "worthiness" hearings might be more of a chance for the military to show off than come off as a full investigation of a whole new concept of war. That, as things turned out, was not too far from the mark. To conduct the hearings a special three-man, one-shot Electronic Battlefield Subcommittee was created with Senators Goldwater and Daniel K. Inouye serving as members and Howard W. Cannon as Chairman.

ELECTRONIC SHOW AND TELL

Come November 18, the first of three days of hearings, the Pentagon brought down some of its newly developed sensors and laid them out on the table for the Senators to see. The initial presentation was something like a rerun from the Mr. Wizard TV show with the gee-whizzing lad sitting at his knee, bedazzled with the glories of modern science:

Senator Goldwater: Does that beep at regular intervals?
General Deane: Just when it detects something, but right now, because there is so much disturbance here, it keeps beeping.

Those disturbances being picked up by the Senators in the hearing room were remarkably positive, even adulatory, and as he had done so many times on the Senate floor Goldwater led the gleeful, Christmas morning chatter. Before the first witness hit the stand, Goldwater proclaimed, as he had on several previous occasions, that it could possibly be one of the greatest steps forward in warfare since the invention of gunpowder.

Such expectations were confirmed by a line of military men who testified to the lethal merits of the electronic battlefield as applied in Vietnam—how, as already mentioned, it came into play at the battle of Khe Sanh, made more accurate the random Harassing and Interdiction program (which wags have translated as firing blind into the jungle), and how it saved American lives. The sensors, placed around American encampments, provided an early warning that even made the cooks more confident, according to General Williamson, who recounted one raid: "I think I have never seen a more confident group of cooks in my life, who, after eliminating some 78 of the enemy in one night, boasted that hot breakfast was served right on time the next morning."

The testifying officers proffered many such moments of high performance for the sensors that detected the enemy and the weapons sent to destroy them, stories that seemed to bring back for a time the glories of past wars not usually associated with Vietnam—only this time the heroes were not men but machines. For instance, the sensors were the real heroes of the Fire Base Crook saga that was retold most enthusiastically by Williamson following this warm introduction, "Now I guess probably the best real war story that I have is the one called Fire Base Crook. This is the story of where some 412 enemy soldiers were eliminated with the loss of only one United States soldier." All through the hearings the talk centered on incidents where hundreds of the enemy died with slight or no American losses. "In all, on the second night," went one part of the Fire Base Crook testimonial, "323 additional enemy were killed and 10 live prisoners taken. I had to move two additional bulldozers up to the area to bury the dead."

Besides war stories, a number of other considerations were discussed. The military men talked about expanding and refining the system for use elsewhere, like Europe, and what the problems might be. General Deane, for instance, explained that something new would have to be developed for England: "There are great chalk deposits, a very small distance below the surface of the ground . . . you don't get very good seismic reaction in that kind of soil . . ." They explained that there were domestic uses foreseen for the system beyond use by the United States Border Patrol, which was already using them to spot border crossers.

However, despite all the information that was given some key questions were left unresolved. One was whether or not the sensors could tell the difference between friend and foe, and if they could, how? The investigation hardly brushed on the question and when it did seemed to bring up even more questions.

The closest thing to a satisfactory accounting came when General Deane was asked about the possibility of an electronic My Lai:

You say the sensors won't tell you. And the sensors might give you an indication if over an acoustic sensor you heard voices and determined from the conversation that they were enemy, that is the only way I would know you would be able to tell. Now, when you get into that kind of a problem, you have to bring to bear your knowledge of where your friendly forces are . . . and use your best judgement. I think the commanders that I have known, if they had doubts, they would not fire.

Similarly, little attention was given to malfunctioning, targeting errors, and false alarms, and when it was the answers came out as generalizations that were not followed with more detailed questioning. When the Subcommittee's director of investigations, Ben J. Gilleas, asked Marine Corps Major Jerry E. Hudson, "Did you have much trouble with false alarms?" Hudson answered, "We did later on. The interpretation people did, yes sir. That word has been stricken from the vocabulary. That is now a nontargetable activation." After adding this new term to the growing collection of Vietnam-era military euphemisms, Hudson stepped down without further questioning.

Noticeably absent from the proceedings were any military men who were less than sold on the system or who had a slightly different interpretation of the electronic battlefield's performance in Vietnam. With the exception of Hudson's admission of nontargetable activations, there was hardly a clue to suggest that it was working at less than 100 percent efficiency 100 percent of the time. One witness, Lieutenant General John Norton of the Army's Combat Developments Command, actually reported that he had just returned from Vietnam where he had talked with over 100 commanders about sensors and, "They were all agreed that the fronts that have to be covered . . . can be covered best with the help of sensors. . . ."

It was not as if there were no dissenters. For example, Lieutenant Jeffrey Belden would have offered a different view of things. He was in charge of all sensor operations in the II Corps area from January 1969 to January 1970 and had earlier written to Proxmire directly to outline some of the problems he had observed. The most damaging portion of his letter had to do with supporting his contention that the system was not as cost effective as the leaders in the Pentagon were claiming:

> . . . I know that the MACV [Military Assistance Command Vietnam] is only interested in the positive aspects of the program. However, statistics were frequently misused to exaggerate the value of the system and other methods were used to make the system look better than it actually was. In one briefing statistics were used to show that the system was 99% effective, when in reality it was not more than 50% effective. Every dead body found anywhere near the devices was counted as a "kill" for the sensors, when in reality these men may have been killed in general air or artillery strikes not all connected with information supplied by the sensors.

Another good witness would have been Colonel Mark M. Boatner, recently retired chief of the Army's Concepts and Doctrine Division who was a critic of the automated battlefield concept. One of his main objections appeared in an article he wrote for *Army* magazine: ". . . field headquarters have become so fat with the people needed to man these new electronic wonders and so heavy with equipment that they are practically immobilized."

Given the determinedly positive nature of the hearings, it came as no surprise to anyone that the final report of the Electronic Battlefield Subcommittee was highly laudatory of the sensor system. Among other things the March 1, 1971, report asserted a "dramatic contribution" to the saving of American lives and a "great stride forward" in military technology. However, the strongest praise was reserved for the "extreme" value of the sensors in ground combat where they enabled the United States to:

(a) deny the enemy the traditional cloaks of bad weather, jungle and darkness;
(b) surprise the enemy and cause him increased casualties and materiel damage;
(c) locate the enemy with sufficient accuracy to permit effective engagement by artillery instead of troops on the ground;
(d) prevent the enemy from disrupting our lines of communication through costly mining operations;
(e) track enemy movements in the so-called 'rocket belts' around major cities and installations to preempt rocket attacks from taking the lives of our servicemen; and
(f) significantly improve the security of United States installations.

This patent medicine box style listing of the conditions cured by the electronic battlefield was typical of the tone of the 20-page report that contained nary a truly negative word on the system.* The furthest it got from unbridled enthusiasm was to suggest that the Army proceed cautiously in adding new elements to its Integrated Battlefield Control System and that various services make sure that they are not duplicating each others' efforts in the field of remote sensor technology.

About the only surprise in the report was that the total appropriated for the electronic battlefield—defined here as "new sensor surveillance equipment" and their associated munitions—

---

* One of the most remarkable kudos to be given to the electronic battlefield was contained in a press release put out by Senator Cannon when the hearing testimony was made public. It read, "Cannon said he was pleased to learn that this program had not experienced any cost overrun." This was a very easy trick since there were never any original estimates to overrun or at least none that were ever made public. If, however, one counts the original Jason/McNamara estimate of a billion dollars, then there was a huge overrun.

was $3.25 billion, and while some $678 million of that total had not been used for the automated battlefield per se, even the resulting $2.63 billion was well in excess of both the $1.68 billion claimed by the military and the $2 billion claimed by Proxmire. As was pointed out earlier, the record shows that this extra $678 million given to the DCPG was turned over to the three services on a "no-strings-attached basis" when DCPG found it did not need the money.

In what was to amount to his last major statement on the subject, Proxmire spoke out later in the month, March 23, to respond to the investigation and the final report of the Subcommittee. After thanking his colleagues for uncovering much new information, he alleged that they had merely lifted "a corner of the veil of secrecy" that had surrounded the program since its inception and said that he could not share his fellow Senators' enthusiasm for the electronic battlefield. More specifically, the conclusions that Proxmire drew from the hearings were that much money had been wasted, especially on Igloo White; that more than the Subcommittee uncovered had been spent on the program; that future program costs may be far in excess of the $150 million a year forecast by the Subcommittee; and that both Congress and the Pentagon were going to have to make sure that future electronic battlefield efforts were well managed and monitored.

With each of these conclusions he supplied the facts that led him to his position. For instance, on the matter of the program attracting more than the $3.25 billion in appropriations uncovered by the Subcommittee, he cited a number of areas where he thought extra costs were lurking. Included were the costs of turning over the sensors and associated equipment to the South Vietnamese, specially equipped aircraft for sensor delivery and the costs of making the sensors available to other friendly nations.

Proxmire and the Subcommittee agreed, however, that the electronic or automated battlefield represented a whole series of technologies and programs that were combining to form a totally new American way of war, and that the investigation had only touched on one part of the whole. In other words it was a classic tip of the iceberg situation that seemed to be begging for deeper examination, or, at the very least, some sort of clear definition of the size of the thing along with an annual review of where it was drifting.

As it turned out, the report and Proxmire's rebuttal actually comprised an end to rather than an early stage in Congressional interest in the subject. Just about all that has followed has been in the nature of adding footnotes, anticlimax, and occasional light questioning in the military committees. For instance, the General Accounting Office report that Proxmire had ordered came out in June and did a competent enough job of adding bits and pieces to the picture—that, for example, the United States was supplying sensors to Australian troops, that the United States Marines were so sold on sensors that from then on each Marine division would travel with a 40-man sensor unit—but interest in it was only momentary and it sparked no new questions from the Hill.

The only act of real significance to come from Congress was the disbanding of DCPG, a group whose presence had begun to irk key members of the House and Senate. One item that bothered them was the $678 million that DCPG had doled out to the Army, Navy, and Air Force without coming to Congress. After all, letting an upstart like DCPG have that much power over the purse was too much even for those who were 100 percent behind what the group had accomplished. In December 1971 the full Senate Armed Services Committee decided to have a look at some of the irregularities in military spending and at the top of the list of things to be examined was the DCPG $678 million. There were many pages of often confusing testimony taken on the tortuous course of the reallocated millions, but when it was all over it was found that some of the money had "lost its identity" and could not be traced to a program or purchase, some had been used for hardware as diverse as rifles and forklift trucks, and some was "reprogrammed back" into electronic battlefield efforts to cover ". . . unforeseen requirements and program changes." In other words, a sizable portion of the millions that DCPG was taking bows for having "saved" in the name of the American taxpayer was passed on for others to spend on DCPG's electronic battlefield. Proxmire's continuing suspicion that costs were hidden was again confirmed.

While the misplaced millions paved the way for DCPG's dismantling, its actual demise was ordered by Congress when it began moving into new realms. On December 12, 1970, less than a month after the Senate Electronic Battlefield hearings, Deputy Defense Secretary David Packard ordered the group to expand its activities from Southeast Asia, where the individual services were taking over sensor operations, to the rest of the world, especially Europe. He also put an open end on the group's possible operations by saying that it would ". . . undertake special high priority development and/or production efforts as directed or approved by the Secretary of Defense." This came after DCPG chief General Lavelle had told Congress that his group would disband once the sensor program was turned over to the services, something he promised would occur before the summer of 1971. Neither Packard's order nor an April change in the name of the group to Defense Special Projects Group (DSPG) were reported to Congress. So, when the Defense Department came to Congress for $34 million in fiscal 1972 funds for DSPG *née* DCPG, the reception was hostile and included, among other things, questions indicating that some actually believed that the name had been changed to hide the group from Congress. When finally worked out between the two Houses only a third of the $34 million requested was approved, and this amount was to be specifically used to finish transferring the sensor system to the services and to finish work on the prototype European version of the electronic battlefield. Moreover the DCPG/DSPG was to close down no later than July of 1972. It performed its last major task, the Mystic Mission display in Germany, in May 1972.

The rationale for killing DCPG was presented in the final fiscal 1972 report of the House Appropriations Committee:

The attempt to maintain this organization with its authorized strength of 164 military and 50 civilian personnel is a classic example of bureaucratic empire building and of the bureaucratic tendency to never end an organization even after the work for which it was created has been concluded. There is no more reason to have a separate organization involved in the management, and what is really the promotion, of remote sensor systems than there is to have a special organization in the Office of the Secretary of Defense devoted to anti-submarine warfare, or close air support, or strategic missiles, or any of a great number of other specific programs. The coordination of the remote sensors program can be easily absorbed within the very large organization of the Director of Defense Research and Engineering.

As logical as it was to close DCPG, the action had a major drawback in that it led to the impression that the electronic battlefield had somehow gone away or, at least, had become nothing much more than a routine interest on the part of the three services in sensor technology. Nothing was further from the truth. By removing DCPG Congress had simply removed a central door to knock on to find out what was happening in regard to the electronic battlefield—a situation tailor-made for new growth. During the 1972 House Appropriations hearings Representative Jamie L. Whitten said to a DCPG representative, "Last year, my recollection is that you told the Congress you were planning to phase this operation out, and Congress agreed to phasing it out. Instead you have changed the name, enlarged it, and now the world is your playground." Ironically, the playground became easier to build without the DCPG, which had become something of a red light to legislators like Whitten and Proxmire.

SIX

Sensory Awareness

. . . as Blue becomes more successful in containing the attack, sensor intelligence verifies Orange's loss of momentum and indicates probable weaknesses in his defensive posture. Timely assessment of sensor intelligence is a valuable adjunct to counter-offensive planning and subsequent action.

PHASE III

Blue initiates a major counter-offensive. Sensors are used to cover the routes leading into objective areas, to screen the front and flanks of advancing units and to monitor the known or suspected locations of Orange units and air facilities . . . new sensor fields are established and old fields are seeded to provide continued sensor emissions for information to both air and ground commanders. . . .

Sensors are also very useful in airborne and special forces operations. . . . As the battle progresses, sensors become a primary source of intelligence showing Orange's redeployment of forces to counter the airborne unit's progress. . . .

Blue ground forces are able to continue their successful counter-offensive. Orange retreats to strong defensive positions in his own territory but is reluctant to negotiate a cease fire.

Orange had not committed major elements of his reserve forces and now decides to undertake a major attack in another sector well south of the primary battle area. His plan calls for a rapid redeployment and a surprise attack by the majority of his forces. The objective is this city. Capture will provide a springboard for a further move to the north. The sensors that Blue has implanted deep in Orange's territory and his current reconnaissance efforts indicate intense activity. In addition, the sensors behind his screening forces begin to reflect the movement of Orange ground forces to the south. . . . To achieve surprise, movements of the Orange forces are made at night or in [bad] weather while observing strict radio and camouflage discipline.

The Blue forces had attained a high degree of air superiority. In addition, they have been actively engaged in reconnaissance, interdiction and close air support. The contained advance of Orange forces is reflected by sensors. . . .

Blue's preparatory action on the ground plus the attrition inflicted on Orange's reserves and the overall loss of tactical surprise enable containment of this crucial campaign at its outset. We will assume Orange seeks negotiations at this point and a cease fire is effected.

PHASE IV

During the cease fire, long-life sensors emplaced in Orange territory continue providing key intelligence inputs. This information . . . enables the Blue force to evaluate and assess the disposition, strength, and probable intent of the Orange force. Sensors in Orange territory are especially important during the critical early phases of a cease fire, when other sources of intelligence may be restricted, by identifying Orange movements that signal a redistribution of his strength.

—*Small portion of the script used in narrating a scale model, table-top war presented as part of the Mystic Mission demonstration, 1972.*

ELECTRONIC BATTLEFIELD I

Should you ask an officer in the Pentagon or someone else with more than a passing knowledge of things military to tell you what the electronic battlefield is, you are liable to get one of two different answers. They are:

Electronic Battlefield I—The first is a very limited definition that grows directly from the hardware developed by DCPG. Those who so apply the term electronic (or automated) battlefield are talking about a collective military effort now counted in the millions rather than in the billions of dollars, and which is strictly limited to the refinement, expansion, and wider deployment of the sensor technology used in Southeast Asia; specifically, unattended ground sensors.

Electronic Battlefield II—The much bigger and more ambitious Westmorelandian vision of a revolution in conventional warfare spelled out in terms of advanced communications, laser arms, sensors, automated fire control systems, remotely piloted aircraft, highly advanced tactical and logistic computer systems, and more. This is a heady dream with a stiff price tag that had already cost more than a billion by the end of 1975 and showed every sign of continuing to rise vigorously. As with version I, those who enjoy this vision use the terms automated and electronic battlefield more or less interchangeably.

From what I can best determine, it is the second or EB II that now comes more commonly to mind when the term is mentioned in military circles, among contractors, and to the press. Articles about the "electronic battlefield" appearing in 1975 in *Time*, *Newsweek*, and *The New York Times* were clearly concerned with EB II. On the other hand, EB I seems to be the more powerful vision in Congress and, naturally, among sensor specialists.

As the rest of the book shows, the author uses the EB II definition, but is also very interested in the more limited first version. So, before moving on to the grander military vision of the future, let us take a look at the linking pin to the larger dream that is a complete vision for some.

The beginning of EB I's saga outside Vietnam dates back to the late days of DCPG. Having had great impact on the technology of jungle war in general and on the Southeast Asian War in particular, DCPG was given one more major job before going out of business. Under the specific orders of Secretary of Defense Melvin Laird, DCPG began work on a project with the code name Mystic Mission at the beginning of 1971. The goal of Mystic Mission was to get the sensors and related equipment into improved, streamlined shape for their European debut. Shortly after getting this assignment, DCPG had its name changed to the Defense Special Projects Group (DSPG.)

As with its first effort, things moved quickly on Mystic Mission. By November 1971 a test of a "Europeanized" system was conducted at Eglin Air Force Base in Florida. It was impressive enough to attract the cosponsorship and cofinancing of the German military for a major demonstration to be held in Germany in 1972. Pulling the Germans in was important in that Congress was increasingly bothered by the tabs that DCPG was running up and the fact that the United States might have to foot the bill for virtually giving away a new weapons technology to Western Europe.

The big Mystic Mission spectacular was set up for the 7th Army Training Center in Hohenfels, Germany, for May 1972. Seven full demonstrations were put on for about 1,000 military officers, defense ministry and NATO staff people, and electronics manufacturers. From the opening moments of each demonstration, there was little question that the United States was intent upon seeing sensor technology jump the Atlantic. One of the first things read at each demonstration was a telegram from Defense Secretary Laird to his top European commander which said in part:

I REGRET THAT MY SCHEDULE WILL NOT PERMIT ME TO ATTEND THE MYSTIC MISSION DEMONSTRATION. MY ABSENCE IN NO WAY INDICATES A LACK OF INTEREST OR ENTHUSIASM FOR THE CAPABILITIES WHICH YOU WILL SHOW OUR NATO ALLIES. I AM CONVINCED THAT SENSOR TECHNOLOGY WILL HAVE SIGNIFICANT APPLICATION IN EUROPE. PLEASE CONVEY TO ALL THE ATTENDEES MY REGRETS AND MY WHOLEHEARTED BELIEF IN THE CAPABILITIES BEING DEMONSTRATED.

In keeping with the rich DCPG heritage and $17 million bill for the Mystic Mission preparations, the final show was hardly a miserly affair. The special secret exhibit area contained a briefing facility where a multi-media show on sensor technology was the featured attraction (background music, slides, film strips, sound effects, and so forth). There were a number of specially built outdoor exhibits, a large field demonstration area replete with bleachers from which to watch the live performance, and an exhibit hall containing 35 colorful booths each of which was designed to show off a piece of the system. This latter pavilion was officially called the "Country Fair" area—aptly named in light of the fact that the United States was admittedly trying to stimulate sensor commerce in an atmosphere not all that unlike a World's Fair midway.

Besides the predictable hardware modifications to accommodate colder temperatures, winter camouflage, and the like, the Hohenfels show provided an excellent opportunity to show off some new gadgets, improvements, and new ideas that had not been ready in time for Vietnam, had been tested there on a limited basis, or were still in advanced development.

One calculated show stopper was a pair of "special devices" created as options for the sensor system. Quoting directly from the 1972 briefing, here is how these two made their debut:

One . . . is the covert observation device which consists of a command transmitter, a covertly emplaced field unit and a receiver station. The field unit is a low-light-level TV camera which can be emplaced in an area of tactical interest.

The field unit may be emplaced near sensors which alert the operator of activity in the area. Upon command, the field unit takes pictures and transmits them to the receiver station where a Polaroid picture is taken and analyzed.

The other special item is the remote firing device which can be used in conjunction with tactical sensors and with the covert observation device. The remote firing device consists of a command monitor unit and a mine firing unit. Up to six strings of munitions, such as anti-personnel mines, can be pre-positioned along an enemy avenue of approach and selectively detonated as required.

The former Covert Observation Device, COD for short, is able to take and transmit pictures from places illuminated with as little light as that given off by a quarter moon.*

But there was so much to behold at the Mystic Mission sensor show that one hardly knows where to begin. One group of innovations only concerned placing the sensors. There was a new, hard-nosed case for implanting sensors in frozen ground, an airborne 8-sensor dispenser from which the sensors were ejected by explosive charge, and the first official announcement of a program for developing techniques for delivering sensors in highly defended areas by means of remotely piloted drone aircraft. Most intriguing, however, was the Artillery Delivered Sensor (ADS), which was revealed as a speedy and accurate means of placing sensors at distances up to eight or nine miles by shooting them out of a standard 155-mm. howitzer. Ingeniously, a special fused charge ejects the sensor from the rear of the shell at the designated drop point. With the help of fins and a braking system it is carefully guided into the ground where it is expected to work for about 60 days.

As always, however, the stars of the show were the sensors themselves and they came in all sorts of new shapes, sizes, and configurations. Infrared sensors, which had been an early DCPG flop, were presented here as operating devices capable of such feats as detecting, counting, and determining the direction of people and vehicles. One, the MIR for Medium Range Infrared Intrusion Detector, was announced here as an item under development, which when perfected would be able to find a man at 60 yards and a truck from almost 300 yards. And by calling this a "Medium Range" instrument, the clear implication was that a "Long Range" was within the state of the infrared art or close to it.

Besides advanced versions of the kinds of sensors that had

---

* The official acronym for the second item, the antipersonnel attachment, is RFD for Remotely Firing Device. Like COD this also comes straight from the post office and must be regarded as a cruel and grim play on the term Rural Free Delivery.

been readied or attempted for the war, Mystic Mission also afforded DSPG an opportunity to show off the latest in American "security" sensors. These were developed by the various services in the late 1960s to stem the rash of assaults on such critical areas as military bases, important buildings, and arms storage areas for reasons of theft and sabotage. Three American bases in the Pacific—two in the Philippines and one in Korea—boast between 300 and 700 sensors as sentries. There are two basic types of "security" systems of which one is an internal system for enclosed spaces like weapons storage rooms within larger buildings. Magnetic switches (tripped when a door or window opens), a warbling alarm (to hear that something is up), and ultrasonic sensors (which detect movement in the room by filling it with a steady tone, high above the level of human hearing, which responds to motion); all report to a central point to tell what is happening in the room. The second type is for outdoor use and is made up of "line" sensors, created to detect intrusion across a line, which are placed end to end to surround a base, building, airport or whatever. A number of techniques are used to locate people crossing the line including a pressure-sensitive liquid-filled hose, a magnetic line for spotting armed intruders, and a special vibration-sensing device to pick up a person climbing on or cutting fence wires.

Cutting across the whole sensor field were some new developments promising leaps forward in longevity and adaptability. What was termed "the greatest single improvement" by MITRE's C. L. Woodbridge was the vastly improved sensor batteries. To cite just one such advance, the standard mercury batteries in the early sensors did not work at low temperatures but a new lithium-organic electrolyte all-weather battery was presented as being able to work at temperatures down to $-20°F$. Another major development was a line of stackable modules, or standardized pieces common to most of the sensors, which made their production a simple by-the-numbers proposition, even in the field.

It was said that these modules would cut production costs, simplify supply procedures, and increase flexibility. Gone, of course, were the deceptive antennae that looked like jungle weeds; in their place were mock-ups of how the detectors would blend into the European landscape, masquerading as fence posts, rotting logs, and rusting metal boxes attached to phone poles that looked as if they belonged there.

For those looking for entirely new sensor departures there were items like DAVID (Directional Acoustic Vehicle Intrusion Detector), a classified entry that presumably yields what its name says it does, a trio of special sensors for locating low-flying aircraft and helicopters, and a very tiny sensor called the MISER (MIni-SEnsor Relay).

Finally on the sensor front was a new generation of sensor combinations and techniques that differed from their fathers in that they were not only able to sense *something* but say what that *something* was. For instance, the advanced "4-Class Seismic Classifier" automatically sorts out what it senses into the category of false alarm, human being, wheeled vehicle, and tracked vehicle. An advanced magnetic sensing technique was unveiled that can remotely discriminate an M-60 from an M-48 tank or a 2.5-ton from a 5-ton truck, and this was the debut of a new acoustic sensor programmed to accept only one target type, such as a tank.

Beyond the sensors themselves there seemed to be an endless array of expensive electronic systems "glue" to hold it all together. If, for example, you were here shopping for something a little less expensive and smaller than the huge operations center used with Igloo White, there was a highly mobile, tactical air control center that took about four hours to set up and to go with it a small Sensor Reporting Post containing the gear needed to monitor, display, and adjudge the pulses of up to 400 individual sensors. And for just a few dollars more you could have a transportable Sensor Assembly and Checkout Shelter ideally suited for setting up your own sensor production line in the field. For someone in the market for a truly mobile unit there was an M-557 armored personnel carrier modified to function as a command post.

The real meaning of the Mystic Mission and its rich collection of hardware was not just that the electronic battlefield had come out of the jungle and was now groomed for the European environment—although this counted for a lot—but that it was ready for the whole world. As Colonel C. J. Lowman, Jr., until recently with the Land War Office at the Department of Defense Office of Research and Engineering (DDR&E), explains, "Europe presents some of the toughest challenges found anywhere for a system of this type, so if it can be made to work there it will work most anyplace." Those European factors include a much more technically sophisticated opponent than was found in Southeast Asia, far less freedom to operate (and drop sensors) in what the Air Force calls the "tactical airspace," and use of radio frequencies that are so intense that it makes the potential for interference greater than in any part of the world. MITRE's Woodbridge sums up what was done in light of these challenges: "We created a generation of 'smarter' sensors backed up with better, more elaborate display and communications equipment to go with it."

While it would take something on the order of a non-nuclear land war between NATO and the Warsaw Pact nations to actually prove or disprove the DSPG/Pentagon claims for what the system could do once it was fully refined and installed, the United States could hardly be faulted for not casting any doubts on its abilities to perform in Europe. The best example of official enthusiasm was expressed in the fictional scale model, table-top demonstration of the system in operation, which was quoted at the beginning of this chapter. While that excerpt gives the flavor of the total script, it is only by following the whole thing that one can see the degree to which the sensor has been given the almighty power to turn the tides of battles and win wars. In the dramatization the sensor-equipped Blue forces gain the upper hand again and again over the sensor-less Orange forces whose "ground and tactical air forces outnumber Blue forces by a substantial margin." Time after time, the hapless Orangemen go on the offensive and are trounced as the vast array of Blue sensors betray their every move. Even at other times, whether it be to interdict Orange supply convoys on their way to the front or to keep a thumb on the pulse of hostile Orange intentions during the cease-fire, sensors, not soldiers, are at the heart of things.

CRICKETS

On June 30, 1972, shortly after the Mystic Mission demonstration ended, DSPG shut down operations and what had come to be known as the sensor community no longer had its Vatican. Sensors and sensor technology had hardly gone out of style and individual EB I organizations continued to operate in various defense installations around the country, but there was no central body in existence to promote and coordinate post–DCPG sensordom. This continued for more than two years until October 1974 when the Cricket Society came into being. Harry Peters, Cricket Secretary-Treasurer and a civilian with the United States Army's Mobility Research and Development Center (MRDC), says, "We're just people who have gotten together to further sensor technology and to informally coordinate sensor-related activities. There are a lot of different types involved, but we are all pretty much agreed that sensors have a major role to play and we all want to make sure that they do."

The reason for the cricket? The Society's vice-president Lieutenant Colonel R. R. Darron, USMC, explains, "When the current generation of sensors are triggered they make a 65-millisecond chirp. Not only does this chirp sound like a cricket, but the sensor itself is like a cricket in that it chirps loudest when agitated." Darron and other Crickets acknowledge that there is another reason for using a mascot in the Society's title, which is that it is patterning itself on another group with a mascot in its

title, the Association of Old Crows. Formed in 1963, the Crows act
as a booster group for electronic warfare (EW), which is that rich
collection of esoteric equipment used to electronically detect,
mislead, and evade enemy weapons efforts. They enjoy an almost
legendary reputation in military circles for what they and their network of chapters (called roosts) have accomplished in creating a
strong and burgeoning market for EW hardware. Like the Crows,
the nascent Cricket Society is open to people from government
and industry and will have chapters dotted across the country.

One of the main things the Crickets will be out plumping for is
more money for their favorite device, thereby enabling it to get
back to what one member terms "the technological foreground."
To hear a Cricket it would seem that this technology was going to
seed. The reason given is that the annual expenditure for sensor
research and development is under the $50 million level as of the
fiscal 1976 budget.* This is, of course, a far cry from the amounts
consumed during the salad days of DCPG. Still, the facts suggest
that the alarm being chirped by the Crickets is a false one—or,
non-targetable activation in their jargon. Sensors are still very
much a going, growing concern of the military, which is not only
catching up with and absorbing the vast outlay of sensor research
and innovation that came out of DCPG but is moving into new
areas as well. Procedures for using them have been introduced
into the operations of all the services and there are literally more
than a dozen military locations nationwide where sensor work is
progressing.

The Army, for instance, is deeply involved with its spearhead
effort, Project REMBASS (Remotely Monitored Battlefield Sensor System), which came into being in May 1971 and which, as of
this writing, was about to present the blueprint for the basic Army
sensor system for the 1980s. Colonel Robert J. Cottey, REMBASS

* As sensor money is spread out and does not show up as such in line items in the
budget, this is about as close as one can hope to come to a current total.

project manager, explains what is in store: "Two areas of major advance will be target classification and target location. I can't go into detail but what I mean by classification is that the sensor's logic will judge and screen material at its end rather than passing it all along and saturating the operator. The target position location capacity just means that we are perfecting the sensor's ability to locate exactly where the target is even if it is some distance from the sensor." (Another Army sensor expert adds that the concept employed is triangulation in which two sensors pinpoint a target at the third corner of a triangle.) The few other public details on what REMBASS is doing include the fact that it is continuing to work on sensor batteries able to operate at low temperatures (the lithium batteries prepared for Mystic Mission had to be refined as the lithium produced a gas that over time caused some sensors to explode), and to do further work on frequency and transmission problems, and considerable anticipatory work on countering efforts to spoof sensors. One particularly novel approach to sensor delivery, which has already been developed, is a "non-implant" system used when dropping sensors from low, slow helicopters. It is "self-orienting" because when it hits the ground it deploys its own seismic transducer and sets up its own antenna. In all, some 36 items—from new sensors to a special training simulator—have been developed by REMBASS and its 16 contractors. The early evidence suggests that the Army will find pleasure in REMBASS' work as it has already committed itself to the purchase of 8,600 REMBASS-developed Platoon Early Warning Systems, each of which is a complete system including eight sensors.

The Army has also been keeping busy with another sensor-heavy effort with still another awkward acronym. J-SIIDS (for Joint-Service Interior Intrusion Detection System) is basically an integrated collection of sensors that detect the penetration of, motion in, and the disturbance of objects within arms rooms and other interior spaces. Thousands of arms rooms are now being outfitted with J-SIIDS as new, more sophisticated "add-ons" to the basic system are developed. The Air Force, on the other hand, is involved in a major effort to develop BIDS (Base Intrusion Detection System) to protect the sanctity of larger installations such as air fields.

And there is still more. An Air Force effort is underway in the tactical area which, according to one well-placed Cricket, is so sensitive that even its name is classified. A guess as to what this project involves would be that it is an attempt to create the new "air-supported barrier" that has been on the Air Force "want list" for several years and is spoken of wistfully in that service's manual on sensors, *Tactical Air Force Operations Operational Concept for Ground Sensor Technology.* The idea goes quite a bit beyond Igloo White in terms of sophistication and efficiency. As envisioned, it would permit the United States to draw a line with sensors, mines, and strike aircraft over which nothing would move—essentially it is a perfected, highly automated version of the McNamara Line, which can be created without putting a single man on the ground. Also, the Air Force has let it be known that it wants sensors able to pipe their signals directly into the fire control systems of strike aircraft to make the whole process nearly instantaneous and much more accurate.

Meanwhile, under the code name Avid Guardian, a trinational effort (the United States, West Germany, and Great Britain) is underway to pick up where Mystic Mission left off and to develop a Europeanized version with expanded capabilities which will be ready for the 1980s. Regardless of support from the rest of NATO, it would seem that a new European system is in the cards. Testifying in support of the fiscal 1974 military R&D budget, the director of the Advanced Research Projects Agency said that while the other nations were making up their minds the United States would go ahead with the development of a new package.

Not to be forgotten in all of this talk of research and development and the shape of the electronic battlefield of the future is the fact that today's forces are truly primed for sensor war. The Marines are a good case in point because they have become most avid users. Initially they began their formal look at the devices through Project STEAM (Sensor Technology as Applied to the Marine Corps), which saw them tried in exercises and tests ranging, geographically, from Norway to the Philippines and, operationally, from desert to amphibious warfare.* Special groups called SCAMPs (Sensor Control and Management Platoons) were created in mid-1970 and became a permanent part of each division. Each SCAMP has two officers, 43 enlisted men, and 720 sensors. According to official Marine doctrine, sensors have become major pieces of combat equipment that add ". . . new dimension to both the quality and quantity of combat intelligence available to Marine commanders."

Of course, it has taken more than new technology per se to exact such dedication from the hard-nosed Marines. The extra factor has been what was actually done with the devices in Southeast Asia beginning with their very successful debut with the Marines at Khe Sanh. However, unlike the Army and its Fire Base Crook and other incidents, and the Air Force's Igloo White, the Marines tended to brag less about their experiences at press conferences and to do more of it internally. Only because of the recent declassification of certain documents can we begin to appreciate the lethal uses to which the Marines put their sensors. As a reconnaissance tool sensors were fine instruments just as capable of helping roll up kill totals for the Marines as for the bragging Army. One incident took place in the An Hoa Basin area

---

* An odd wrinkle came about early in the Marines' testing which showed off the sensors (but not the Marines) to good advantage. During Exercise Bell Call at Camp Pendleton, California in March of 1969, the men monitoring the sensors picked up activity late at night when nothing was supposed to be going on. The activations were disregarded. The next morning, however, it was discovered that a Southern Pacific freight train had derailed near Fairfield after hitting an open section of track which had apparently been rigged by saboteurs out to slow the flow of munitions destined for Southeast Asia.

near Danang in which sensor-equipped troops of the 1st Reconnaissance Battalion of the 1st Marine Division were able to kill 215 of the enemy with only six wounded Marines and no deaths. Another total that is nearly as impressive was that posted by another Marine unit that killed 110 North Vietnamese and Viet Cong in a month without sacrificing any Americans.

By the Corps' own judgment, however, the most noteworthy success of all came in a sensor-supported action called the "Air Ambush." To relate just one final example of EB I in action, here is what happened in a successful application of the concept southwest of Danang. It must be considered a most chilling example of sensors in action because of the degree to which it begins to describe in real life Westmoreland's 1969 vision of small units presiding over killing zones from which it is almost impossible to escape.

The ambush in question was organized by a reconnaissance patrol of the 1st Marine Division in response to irksome and persistent enemy foot traffic through the valley. Here is a graphic description found in Marine Corps papers which have only recently lost their "CONFIDENTIAL" markings:

Overlooking the valley from a vantage point, the patrol monitored seismic devices, while the patrol's FAC [Forward Air Controller] maintained radio contact with all aviation elements involved. A flight of A-6A's orbited well to the north of the ambush, while an OV-10A carrying an airborne FAC was on station to the east. At a combat base seven miles to the west of the trap an ASRT [Air Supported Radar Team] was standing by to provide radar-controlled bombing guidance. Additional attack aircraft, on strip alert status, were on call from the Danang Air Base. Movement in the target area was indicated by the seismic detectors, whereupon the use of NOD's [Night Observation Devices] confirmed over 60 enemy moving eastward on a direct approach to the killing zone. Leading the target by selecting an impact point ahead of the enemy column, the FAC relayed target location coordinates to the ASRT for the first air strike. As the enemy moved forward, the ASRT, utilizing TPQ-10 all-weather radar, vectored the first A-6A on target. Observing the string of 28 five-hundred-pound bombs strike the end of the column the FAC provided an immediate target adjustment, bringing ordnance of the next A-6A's on the dispersing enemy.

As the A-6A's departed the killing zone with a drop of parachute flares, the FAC then called in a flight of three F-4 aircraft which had been launched from Danang when the ambush was triggered. Circling the lighted area, the airborne FAC gave the first F-4 pilot his target, a remnant of the disorganized column. Six enemy running from the initial impact of the napalm were caught in the open as the second aircraft made its delivery. Identified by the airborne FAC, additional targets were hit until all movement in the valley ceased.

As if it were actually needed to underscore what had happened, the document went on to further brag about how the Marines have mastered the technology of shooting fish in a barrel:

The element of total surprise, the coordination between air and ground units, and the innovative use of technological surveillance advances all contributed to the success of the ambush—at least 48 of some 60 NVA soldiers killed. The patrol, able to maintain a covert status throughout the evening, sustained no casualties.

Nor is this the only ambush technique in the Marine Corps repertoire. A newer one, the "mechanical ambush," is based on the use of the aforementioned Remotely Firing Device (RFD), which pretty much eliminates the middleman in killing. The chosen weapon fired with the RFD is the Claymore mine, which is a 3.5-pound curved box sitting on folding legs. The box itself features a fragmentation face (steel balls embedded in plastic) and an explosive charge inside giving it a kill zone the height of a human out to more than 150 feet. The Marines feel that RFDs can be effectively used by troops operating them as much as five miles away. (For members of the TV generation at home with violence on the small screen, but not up for watching other humans turned into mincemeat right in front of them, this is the perfect system when used with the Covert Observation Device (COD) and its low-light level TV.)

Should there still be the slightest question as to the role that ground sensors will play in the next war that the US fights, listen to a key line given by ARPA Director Dr. Stephen J. Lukasik to the House Armed Services Committee on March 7, 1974, concerning the character of war from 10 to 30 years hence: "The tactical world will be dominated by systems that are cheap and widely distributed: or manned portable anti-tank and anti-aircraft weapons, unmanned remotely-piloted vehicles, and unattended ground sensors directly coupled to weapons systems."

Such couplings link the sensor-dominated first version of the electronic battlefield with the grander vision now taking shape. Before moving on to that vision, however, there is another side to the story of sensors worthy of brief attention.

FIRST, A WORD FROM YOUR LOCAL SENSOR

The White House lawn, Disney World, the border between the US and Mexico, an exclusive subdivision in the Maryland suburbs of Washington, and a number of other places and institutions have one thing in common, which is that they are to varying degrees making use of the sensors, night-vision devices and other DCPG-related technology of the Southeast Asian War.

Like their military counterparts, civilian users have, for the most part, not been reluctant to come across with success stories. Army Starlight Scopes have been pressed into service by Park Service rangers to apprehend wrongdoers working at night, such as alligator poachers in the Everglades. A heat sensing camera used to detect traffic along the Ho Chi Minh Trail has been pressed into service (along with the Navy patrol plane that carries it) by the Environmental Protection Agency to spot water polluters. There is a growing collection of stories about night vision devices in police work, which run the gamut from a Boston situation in which a major narcotics transaction was watched in the dark leading to a major arrest to a Linden, N.J., sniper incident in which just prior to the moment that the police opened fire on the suspected gunman the night vision device showed that the man about to be shot was actually another policeman. Los Angeles County firemen now use night-vision goggles as they direct night and low-visibility forest fire fighting operations from helicopters, and, as has been pointed out in a national advertising campaign, an ITT light amplifying device developed for the Army is now used experimentally to help those suffering from retinitis pigmentosa, a blinding disease that often makes it especially difficult for those afflicted to see in dim light. Sensors have been put to use selectively in a number of situations in which the goal is to detect interlopers. They have been used experimentally at airports to head off cargo theft, by a Delaware telephone company to protect against pilferage of copper parts, in selected home security applications such as the aforementioned Maryland suburb, by Customs and Drug Enforcement Administration officials in keeping tabs on the traffic at remote and deserted airstrips, and, according to a report in *Electronics* magazine, by the Secret Service to keep the seismic pulse of the White House grounds. For every actual installation there are a number of proposed civilian sensor applications for such places as nuclear power plants, warehouses, government installations and the like.

Of all the applications of sensors to date, the most ambitious has been the McNamara Line type of border fence erected along portions of the US-Mexican border. This all began in 1969 with the Nixon Administration's Operation Intercept to cut drug smuggling between the two countries. At the time, Intercept Director Eugene T. Rossides pledged that the most modern military equipment would be thrown into the effort including both airborne sensing devices and unattended ground sensors. These early uses of ground sensors were effective and within a year John Mitchell's Justice Department was seeding a 65-mile experimental stretch of the border with Vietnam-tested acoustic sensors, buried strain-sensitive cables, and infrared detection devices. In 1972 when the test section was fully operational 128,889 illegal crossers were apprehended along the stretch, of whom authorities claimed more than 30,000 were netted as a result of the electronic fence. In the fall of 1973 the US Border Patrol and the Immigration and Naturalization Service jointly announced plans to expand the fence along the whole 2,000-mile border with the exception of the most inaccessible areas, and immediately pledged $1.5 million to start the job.

Today electronic sensors are installed at the most active points along the border, but there is some question at the moment whether the whole border will be wired. This situation largely results from the success of the system (although costs have been a factor too). General Leonard F. Chapman, Jr., head of the Immigration and Naturalization Service, explained in a 1975 interview appearing in *Nation's Business* that the sensors work fine but that more than half the alarms go unanswered because the Border Patrol itself is spread so thin.

While most of this military to civilian spin-off of hardware has been benign or downright useful, it does not take much imagination to envision devices plugged in and wired down at such a rate and for such purposes that we are soon at Orwell's nightmare state in which there is ". . . no way of knowing whether you were being watched at any given moment. How often, or on what system, the Thought Police plugged in on any individual wire was guess work. It was even conceivable that they watched everybody all the time." Within such a context, there is a definite chill in such bits of recent news as these:

—The FBI has recently purchased two Army planes equipped with the most sophisticated airborne sensing devices. Some have wondered aloud if this could be the first buy in an FBI airborne surveillance force.

—Increasingly, companies possessing the technology are advocating sensors and associated items for a bigger and more diverse market which should soon get down to the man on the street. The technology is ready. Several companies have devices able to discriminate between humans and pets. Some of the new general market sensors appear to have the capacity to fulfill a Big Brother as well as a crime-stopping role. For instance, a new capacitance proximity sensor from GTE Sylvania responds when one touches or even comes very close to a metal object such as a desk or filing cabinet. One sensor can keep track of 20 desks.

—The police in a number of communities across the country are now able to keep tabs on whole neighborhoods through the use of 24-hour closed circuit TV systems. The first operation of this type was installed in a section of Mount Vernon, N.Y., by Sylvania with the help of a $47,000 grant from the Justice Department. "Only time will tell," said a Sylvania paper on its system, "if citizens will object to a 'Big Brother' type atmosphere." A number of systems have followed but, in terms of the latest in Buck Rogers urban technology, it would seem hard to beat a two-square-mile area on Cleveland's East Side where low-light level color TV images are sped to police headquarters by laser beam.

There can be little question that all of this is proliferating despite its expense. A Star-Tron night vision device for police costs between $3,000 and $5,000 depending on its size, and an expert estimates that the job of sealing the whole Mexican border with sensors will cost hundreds of millions of dollars. To see this proliferation one need only stroll through the hardware display areas of such affairs as the annual International Security Conference or look through the list of current R&D grants from the Justice Department's Law Enforcement Assistance Administration or scan the papers given at the heavily electronics-oriented

Carnahan Crime Countermeasures Conference put on each year by the University of Kentucky. At the Carnahan Conference one is liable to glean any number of leads on the future shape of police electronics, such as a 1973 paper given by researchers from the Plessey Radar Research Center in Great Britain that reported progress on a new sensor for detecting cadavers by sensing decomposition. Just the thing for finding dead bodies. There may be a lead in this for military electronics too as one wonders if perfection of the body sensor might lead to the automated body count. Significantly, some of the financing of this electronic marvel comes from the US Army.

Even more to the point are some of the proposals that are rather routinely made at Carnahan and similar forums for further domestic wiring. A paper from Radiation Incorporated, a major electronic battlefield contractor, talked of and clearly advocated heavily sensoring American communities to keep an electronic vigil on golf courses, shopping centers, construction sites and the like. The author of the paper, Guy H. Smith, Jr., created a mythical Smithville, U.S.A. with a population of 80,000 to 100,000 people, which he felt could be adequately taken care of with a collection of 1,100 assorted sensors. He ended his presentation by predicting that Smithvilles—each replete with an "Environmental Assessment Center" for sorting out the blips—will be "very common" in the future. This apparently does not seem too far fetched to others because a conference paper given by a sensor expert from Sylvania talks of the need for police equipment that will routinely process the output of a thousand or more sensors. Other trial balloons launched at recent Carnahan sessions have included calls for city-wide schemes for infrared and television surveillance and plans for electronically tracking the movement of vehicles and people. When you get into the realm of proposed tracking schemes, there are some especially Orwellian ideas around. A prime candidate for the most startling of all did not appear at the Carnahan conference but in a forum just as august, the journal *Transactions on Aerospace and Electronic Systems.* The article by Joseph Meyer, an engineer in the employ of the National Security Agency, recommends a system in which tiny electronic tracking devices (transponders) are attached to those 20 million Americans who have been in trouble with the law—in fact, wearing one of the devices would be a condition of parole. The transponders would be linked by radio to a computer that would monitor the wearer's (or "subscriber's" in the words of Meyer) location and beep out a warning when the person in question was about to violate his territorial or curfew restrictions. In addition, these little boxes would be attached to people in such a manner that they could not be removed without the computer taking note of the act. Taking off or tinkering with your transponder would, in Meyer's world, be a felony. Good engineer that he is, Meyer has also thought out some of the other applications of these portable units, which include monitoring aliens and political minorities.* Robert Barkan, the writer who first brought the Meyer proposal and other such ideas to a broader audience through his articles, had this to say about the transponder system in *The Guardian,* " '1984' is still fiction, but no longer *science* fiction. The technology of the police state is ready. All that remains is for the government to implement it."

Significantly, almost everyone who has looked into the domestic electronic spin-off from military surveillance technology comes back to *1984.* Unfortunately, however, making comparisons to Orwell's classic does not seem to have quite the same horrific clout it had a few years ago. At the end of the International Security Conference in Washington in 1972, the conference coordinator Art Lilienthal made this telling comment to a reporter from *The Washington Post,* "There was a time when the public was very much upset about 'Big Brother!' Now, the public is beginning to

---

* Similar transponders were tested in Vietnam to keep track of GIs so that they would not be targeted accidentally by American aircraft.

accept this as a fact of life. They recognize, realize, appreciate and accept the fact that Big Brother is not really some alien being, but that he's their friend."

If this is true, then our choices are limited and it is just a matter of time until our options boil down to the extras we will take with our lawn sensors and the color we will choose for the transponder that hangs around our neck. If not, there is still time to heed the implied warning of Orwell's vision as well as other more recent warnings. An appropriate one was a little-noticed caveat that appeared in a 1967 paper of a RAND Corporation systems engineer, Paul Baran, with experience in military and police command and control systems. His thesis is that while new equipment and techniques were needed by law enforcement agencies, it would be easy to go too far and make it too easy to gather information on individuals, which would lead to an intoxication of power, which, in turn, could pave the way for ". . . the most effective, oppressive, police state ever created."

Nearly ten years have passed since Baran's warning, and all the arrows point to the conclusion that it is now more relevant than when it was originally issued. This seems to be so not only because of the tons of electronics gear installed to watch over America in the interim, but also because of the continually remarkable pace of technology. At the time of the Baran paper, today's most effective surveillance instruments were only imagined. An important representative example of what has since been created is a special TV camera for the surveillance market that was announced by the General Electric Company in 1974. It is remarkable on two counts. First, because of its ability to take crisp pictures with no more light than that given off by a single candle, it stands as the world's most sensitive TV camera. Second, it is wallet-sized and weighs less than a pound. For the snoopers, the privacy shattering potential of just this one piece of hardware seems vast.

SUPER-SENSOR. One of the FLIR (Forward Looking Infrared) devices that will soon be found in almost all United States military aircraft. These instruments sense differences in thermal radiation on the ground that are projected on a screen in the cockpit. They work both day and night and under all weather conditions. (Hughes Aircraft)

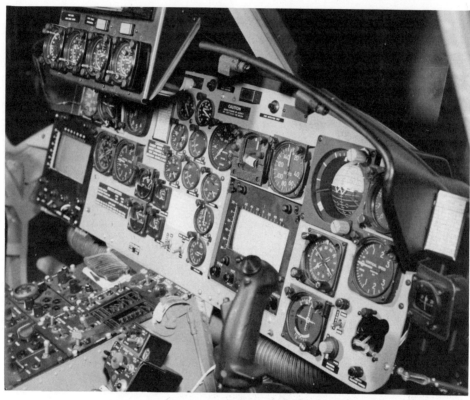

NEW FACE OF WAR. The two small screens in this helicopter cockpit are used by the pilot and copilot for locating and zeroing in on targets. This is a FLIR system that in one of its several modes of operation can actually be used to direct M21 guns on a target. (Aerojet Electrosystems)

TV GUIDE. The TV-guided "smart" bombs called HOBOS (for HOming BOmb Systems), which were used with such devastating effect during the waning days of the Vietnam war, are shown in exhibit and slung beneath two F-4 Phantom jets on their way to a mission. (Rockwell International)

ZAPPER. One of the many new laser systems now being evaluated by the military is the ALLD (Airborne Laser Locator Designator) shown mounted on the stub wing of an Army "Cobra" helicopter. The laser beam marks targets for destruction by laser-guided "smart" bombs, artillery, and missiles. (Philco-Ford)

KETTERING "BUG." The experimental—and not too successful—First World War era craft that first advanced the idea of unmanned military flight. (U.S. Air Force Museum, Dayton, Ohio)

"ROLLOUT." The most ambitious of the RVPS now flying is the Air Force's experimental Compass Cope shown here as two Teledyne Ryan prototypes made their official debut in January 1974. Unlike other early RPVs that are launched from a manned mothership and snagged on their return by a helicopter, these aircraft have landing gear for automated takeoff and landing. (Teledyne Ryan)

ALOFT. One of the prototype Compass Cope aircraft in test operation. The plane has already proven itself capable of flying for more than 24-hours at a stretch at altitudes in excess of 55,000 feet. (U.S. Air Force photo by James P. Porter)

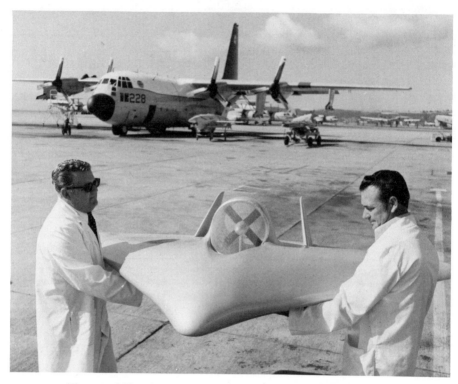

MINI. The portability shown here is a prime feature of the new Mini-RPVs now undergoing development. Another great advantage of this class of aircraft is that because of its size and advanced technology it will be hard for an enemy to see, hear, or pick up on radar. This particular offering is from Teledyne Ryan and measures only $7\frac{1}{2}$ feet from wingtip to wingtip. (Teledyne Ryan)

RECYCLING. Sequence shows Air Force DC-130 mothership loaded with a full set of RPVS for midair launch, the launching itself, and helicopter recovery at the end of the mission. For reasons of size and economy most of the RPVS of the future will be sent off and brought back in this manner. The "hashmarks" on the fuselage of the "Tom Cat" in the second picture signify previous missions. (Teledyne Ryan)

ROBOT WARRIOR. An Air Force officer checks air-to-surface missile slung from the wing of an RPV. A Mark IV bomb is tucked under the left wing for good measure. Current plans call for considerable weapons delivery work in the future. (Teledyne Ryan)

JACK-OF-ALL-TRADES. Artist's rendering of the proposed Air Force modular, multimission RPV system that will be able to be configured for a number of jobs from weapons delivery to reconnaissance. (Teledyne Ryan)

TINKERING. This picture of technicians preparing a Philco-Ford "Praeire" for flight underscores the extent to which RPV technology is like model aircraft work. The difference between the toys and the RPVs, of course, is that the latter carry a lethal punch. This 60-pound model is intended to carry a payload that includes a laser to guide highly accurate bombs to their targets. (Philco-Ford)

TEST BED. A number of companies are scrambling to get a piece of the RPV action. Here is a modified target drone that Northrop is trying to get the military to buy as a vehicle to test new RPV systems and concepts. The special wingtip pods can be used to carry such extra payloads as communications, electronic warfare or navigation packages. (Northrop)

SENSOR SEEDING. One of the many tasks envisioned for RPVs in the electronic battlefield of the future: vehicles for the delivery of sensors. (U.S. Navy/MITRE)

SUICIDE PLANE. One company's mockup of the Air Force's proposed Tactical Expendable Drone System (TEDS), a cheap, one-way vehicle intended for missions that would be suicidal for a manned aircraft. (Northrop)

SNOW JOB. Air Force men loading a strike RPV in an exercise under less than ideal conditions. The exercise has meaning because as now envisioned RPVs will be used for combat work in all kinds of weather and at night. (U.S. Air Force)

SPECTER OF THE FUTURE. A mothership has just let fly one of her RPVs carrying a TV-guided tactical missile in this ghostly image taken during a 1974 demonstration of the efficacy of the latest in electronic battlefield technology. (U.S. Air Force)

SEVEN

Blipkrieg

> A remarkable series of technical developments has brought us
> to the threshold of what I believe will become a true
> revolution in conventional warfare.
> —*Director of Defense Research and Engineering Dr.*
> *Malcolm R. Currie, testifying before Congress March,*
> *1974.*

ELECTRONIC BATTLEFIELD II

Late in May 1975 an American U-2 aircraft crashed in
Germany while on what was at first only described as a sensitive
mission. On Friday, May 30, *The Washington Post* cited a
Pentagon source that said the plane was participating in work
leading towards the "automated battlefield of the future." The
Post went on to explain that U-2s are flying over known United
States and NATO radars in order to test a new triangulation
system that pinpoints their location even after the briefest
transmission periods. In wartime the system would be used to
locate and destroy enemy radar installations with laser-guided
and other "smart" bombs.

I immediately began calling around to get more details on the
system in the U-2 incident. The first four sources, who were all
closely identified with sensors, that I contacted, knew nothing

159

more than what had appeared in the *Post* and in a follow-up account in *Aerospace Daily*. As an Army engineer put it, "That's not part of our automated battlefield." The "our" in his remark was not a reference to the Army, but to the sensor system. The point demonstrated, of course, was that the first electronic battlefield, or EB I, is a mere parochial subsystem of EB II.

My fifth attempt to learn more about the U-2 system was through a source at the Advanced Research Projects Agency, the official forefront of military technology, who told me that he had heard of the system, that the *Post* article had gone much further than it should have, and that it was doubtful that I would get anything more on it. He added that if I was hoping to write about "the automated battlefield in the large sense of the word" then I would hit a lot of dead ends marked secret, and that I would be lucky if I got a hint of what was going on. The man was clearly right in that certain elements of the battlefield of the future are kept far from public view, and for the layman looking at it all from the outside there are bound to be loose ends, omissions, and imperfections. Despite that, information from Congressional military hearings, other parts of the public record, on the record interviews, the aerospace and military trade press, and other unclassified sources, gives, though the details are missing, a rough rendering of the whole that is stunning.

Where to begin? Perhaps it is best to go back to an interview I had early in 1974 when I was first trying to get some idea of the total immensity of the thing. I spoke to Lieutenant Colonel C. J. Lowman, Jr., who was with the Land War Office of the Department of Defense Office of Research and Engineering (DDR&E). He said that the concept is involved in large development programs in almost every area of defense R&D today, from efforts in automated data processing for tactical applications to new weapons. The idea is no longer tied to the ground as might be inferred from the word "battlefield" but has stretched out to include the oceans and air-to-air combat. When I asked him how much money is involved annually in projects associated with the electronic battlefield, Lowman smiled and said, "I guess you'd have to say that the large majority of the DoD's $9 billion current annual R&D budget is now part of that effort." Even at this rate of at least $5 to $6 billion a year (which is only R&D and does not include those parts of the whole actually being produced) the electronic battlefield has already dwarfed most other huge Federal efforts and should soon be in the price class of the Apollo Program for space exploration.

What the Pentagon is buying for this money is a major transformation which, by the end of the decade, will have given it a new modus operandi, a new set of operating premises and philosophy that it will build on, one can presume, through the end of the twentieth century. This is the "revolution in conventional warfare" talked about by Pentagon planners that will usher in abilities that existed only in science fiction magazines a few years ago. One is a "one-shot one-kill" ability for the next generation of weapons. "Essentially," Pentagon research chief Currie recently explained to *Newsweek*, "we would like for every missile, bomb or shell to kill its target." Another is a quantum jump in the speed and quality of military communications and still another is to automate away just about every routine job in sight. What it all boils down to is a totally new speed and precision in military operations making them much more deadly.

The springboard for this leap into the future is modern electronics, which had penetrated virtually every facet of military operations by the early 1970s and will completely dominate them by the end of the decade. *Air Force*, the official magazine of the Air Force Association, recently said that if electronics had been taken away from the United States during the Second World War, the consequences would have been felt but would not have been major. "Today," it continued, "without its electronic systems, the USAF literally could not get off the ground." Similar electronic coups have been accomplished in the Army and Navy too.

Of course an important key element in all this is sensors, and not just the unattended ground sensors that have dominated the book so far, but sensors in the larger sense of the word meaning any piece of equipment that is used to sense the presence of a prospective enemy. This would include sonar, infrared sensors flying aboard airplanes, special sets of sensors on orbiting satellites, radar, and various photographic devices. So far we have paid little attention to the Navy for the rather obvious reason that, with the exception of certain amphibious warfare applications, it has little use for land-based EB I sensors. Yet when it comes to sensors in the larger sense the Navy is probably the most deeply involved. On the floors of the world's oceans, the Navy now has a broad network of unmanned sensors in place and set to detect the hum of alien submarine engines. Still more sophisticated versions are being developed that hear the very silent Soviet subs, which will be in operation in the 1980s. The Navy is also involved in infrared technology and has announced that it is working on sensors that will be able to note the path of a moving submarine hours after it has passed.

A particularly impressive piece of hardware that the Navy is developing is the Captor (short for en*cap*sulated *tor*pedo), which will be responsible unto itself for when it fires. It consists of a set of sensors and a torpedo locker. The whole unit is anchored to the seabed to await action. When activated at the beginning of hostilities the sensing system will presumably detect enemy submarines and fire its guided "smart" torpedo at the first one that comes within range. A string of Captors properly strewn under the Baltic will, according to Navy experts, be able to stop a lot of Soviet subs on their way to the Atlantic.

An unusual bit of technological showboating on the Navy's part? Not at all. If Captor seems more like a special front-of-the-pack system, consider some of its comrade systems on the very electronic battlefield of the near future: Low flying "cruise" missiles winging their way in under radar level on their way to a target that they, literally, locate by reading a map . . . mines that dig their own holes, cover themselves over and wait for their prey . . . computers able to understand tough tactical questions asked in English and quickly answer in the same tongue . . . Navy surveillance systems routinely able to find and keep track of the other side's submarines up to 6,500 miles away . . . more Captor-like systems that will pick their own targets and fire on them . . . a missile able to detect, lock onto and attack enemy radar installations . . . large cannonlike disintegrator lasers and other bits of "death ray" technology . . . satellites able to attack their Soviet counterparts at the touch of a button on earth . . . soldiers with laser designators no larger than a flashlight able to point their beams at a target and expect artillery shells to come on the scene, find, lock onto, and home in on their beams . . . nearly complete automation of battlefield command and control . . . spaceborne TV cameras of amazing power able to let the White House remotely zoom-in on any part of the globe for live coverage of what is going on . . . location systems so sure-fire that no soldier, sailor, or airman anywhere in the world will be more than a moment away from a portable device that tells him exactly where he is . . . 3-D radar . . . remotely piloted aircraft in all shapes and sizes including a one-way model intended for Kami-kaze missions . . . and more.*

Then there are those highly advanced items and techniques that have already gone into place like the collection of refined sensors aboard Air Force "Big Bird" satellites which, *Time* reported, "are so effective they were able to follow the movement

---

* A number are all but impossible for an outsider to find out about. Here, for example, is the entire description of a new system as it appears in the publicly-distributed fiscal year 1975 Senate Armed Services Committee Hearings: "Another project in the [deleted] is concerned with the development of [deleted] primarily for [deleted] although it is anticipated that this technology, if successful, will find wide application to other military problems. Here we are attempting [deleted]. This requires the development of [deleted]."

of individual tanks across the Sinai desert during the 1973 war."
In some cases, new versions of relatively old concepts like
electronic jamming and counter measure, which has become a
highly advanced science of deceit and mimicry that seems to
become more sophisticated by the day, fit into the picture of the
battlefield of the future.

SHOPPING LIST

The best way to get a more specific feel for what the military
R&D machine is creating is to introduce some of these just-
mentioned technological stars of the future in greater detail.
Though not yet stars as they are in various stages of preparation,
we will nonetheless observe the custom of all-star casts and list
them alphabetically.

Artificial Intelligence—It has been known for a long time that a
certain amount of Pentagon research money is annually ear-
marked for exploratory research into the unnerving realm where
computers go beyond their vast capacity to store and compute
data and begin to perform as "intelligent" entities. However, it
was not until March 1975 when the new Director of the Advanced
Research Projects Agency, George H. Heilmeier, was explaining
what his group's requested 1976 budget would pay for that the
extent of the effort became apparent. The most intriguing thing he
said about the general thrust of the artificial intelligence program
was:

Although the science and technology that has been developed by the
program is by no means mature, it has proven itself to be capable of
supporting significant applications such as problem-solving systems in
mass spectroscopy and nonnumerical mathematics. It has proved to
equal the performance of the best human experts. Several conceptual
demonstrations are now being undertaken in other areas such as
maintenance and repair of electronic circuits, receiving Morse code in

the presence of interference, and making computers respond to ordinary DoD users helpfully and intelligently in natural English instead of the highly demanding and impersonal manner that frustrates the nonprogrammer.

A computer that can actually out-think the experts in an area like mass spectroscopy would appear to be just the beginning. Another effort is moving towards the automated programming of computers by computers, another to have computers replace humans as interpreters of reconnaissance photos and radar images, and still another to yield the "intelligent computer terminal," which will help a human without much knowledge of computers in operating itself. For those of high rank, ARPA is working on a system to aid in decision making on matters related to national security. The assumption here is that in complex military situations it is impossible for even the brightest human to put together all the factors needed to come up with what the Pentagon calls the "optimal rational solution" or, as the rest of us would say, the best answer.

What is probably the most stunning accomplishment to date, however, appeared on a 1974 list of ARPA accomplishments: "The analysis of electroencephalograph signals has been refined to the point where a computer can discern which of a limited set of commands a user is thinking. This research also holds promise of adding a significant new capability to the linkage of man and machine."

For researchers who have already come up with a computer that can begin to read the human mind, the near-term—let alone long-term—possibilities would seem limitless. For one, computers that analyze the behavior and statements of an adversary (or an inconsistent ally, for that matter) can produce an "objective" unemotional appraisal of his intentions. Reading through the computer research objectives sponsored by ARPA and others in the military one only has to do a little reading between the lines to see a not-too-distant future in which there are self-repairing computers, machines that rearrange their own internal logic as advances are made in the programming art, and crisis computers that go beyond helping decision makers in a tight situation and actually dictate the course of action to be taken.

Airborne Warning and Control System (AWACS)—At $111 million per copy, this souped-up Boeing 707 crammed with radars, sensors, computers, and communications equipment will be the most expensive Air Force aircraft ever built. Its most distinguishing physical characteristic is a 30-foot rotating radome (which looks like a giant mushroom) for its special antennae. The purpose of the 31 planes the Air Force is trying to get permission to build will be to provide high-speed flying command posts with special all-altitude surveillance abilities enabling them to keep track of air, ground and sea activities over a large area. Further, backers of the plane claim it would be able to peer deep into enemy territory without flying over it. From the Air Force's standpoint, AWACS is the ultimate battlefield management center.

Largely through the efforts of Senator Thomas Eagleton some questions have been raised regarding this plane, which has already cost over a billion dollars mostly in R&D costs. Eagleton's probing has led to several charges of which the most serious and hardest to shake is that the plane can be jammed with relative ease by Soviet equipment, a contention that has been backed up from other quarters including two critical reports from the General Accounting Office.

The reaction to all this from the Air Force has been to show how well it works in exercises with early demonstration models. A spring 1975 display over the Atlantic Ocean showed it could keep electronic track of over 600 civil and military aircraft and large numbers of ships despite the efforts of two jamming aircraft. Earlier in the same year an AWACS prototype underwent several showy maneuvers in Europe (where, incidentally, NATO allies are considering buying some of their own). In various tests it showed its ability to send its bird's eye information directly to surface forces (such as onto the screen of a ship's radar), to feed target coordinates to ground-based missile batteries, and to pick up planes flying below normal radar with its special "look down" radar. While flying over the North Sea, it showed how it would control close-in battlefield operations while keeping track of air traffic as far distant as Moscow. A few months before the European show, a mock air battle was held in which two AWACS-guided F-15s took on nine attacking planes of which three were to try to jam the AWACS. All nine were picked up about 100 miles away and "shot down" before they had made it half way to the AWACS plane despite some tricky flying on the part of the attackers. One flew close to the ground along the route of a highway attempting to get lost in ground clutter. The AWACS plane picked it up first as what appeared to be a supersonic car.

Criticism of the expensive plane has slowed the pell-mell rush to buy them and the Air Force's planned first production lot of a dozen in its 1975 budget request was cut in half mainly because of the issue of jamming that Eagleton had raised. If the Air Force can show that jamming is not the major problem critics say it is—and it is working overtime to counter this charge—AWACS will become the great electronic mother hen of the electronic battlefield.

Cruise Missiles—These are a new class of surface-to-surface weapons for the United States military which are the modern descendants of the Nazi "buzz" bombs of World War II that terrorized London. Unlike the high-arching, bulletlike ballistic missile, a cruise missile is a low-flying bomb (conventional or nuclear) with air-breathing turbine engines and wings, which can be launched from a plane, ship, or submarine. The main difference between the American versions and the old Nazi models is their sophistication, more specifically their guidance systems that will enable them to pinpoint and hit targets as far as 1,500 miles from their launch site.

The Navy and Air Force have taken a rather sudden interest in these weapons which in part stems from the fact that the Soviets have become increasingly devoted to them—it was a Russian-built cruise missile that sunk the Israeli destroyer *Elath* in 1967—and the US wants to "balance the threat." However, they have an attraction beyond helping the US keep up with the Soviet Union. For instance, here is how Rear Admiral G. E. Synhorst, Assistant Deputy Chief of Naval Operations for Submarine Warfare, summed up the rationale for a submarine-launched cruise missile to the Senate Armed Services Committee: "This system would add a new dimension to our strategic arsenal by providing a low-altitude, low-infrared signature, low-radar cross section cruise missile that could be launched from existing submarine torpedo tubes." He goes on to explain that a large number of them could be dispatched from outside the Soviet defense perimeter to mount a low altitude attack on that country which would "stretch and confound" that nation's defenses.

What is most fascinating about cruise missiles is the terrain-following guidance system now being developed for them. Called TERCOM (for terrain contour matching) the system gives the missile the ability to find a target by reading a digital map. En route, it compares the map to what it electronically senses on the ground it is flying over and makes the proper adjustments. A number of tests have been conducted already allowing a prototype TERCOM system to control a manned A-7 aircraft (in which the man was needed for takeoff and landing) with the amazing result that in 100 approaches to five targets under various conditions of light, weather, and foliage there was not one miss. The targets were no snap either. One, for instance, called for TERCOM to take the plane from the Navy Air Station at Patuxent River, Maryland, and find the Burlington, Vermont Municipal Airport.

It was also sent out to find a spot in a distant part of Canada in winter to see if heavy snow on the ground would somehow confuse it. It did not.

These missiles will allow the military to make a great leap forward in what it terms "standoff ability", which means fighting the good fight from a safe distance. Now pilots and submariners will be able to "drop" bombs with no more danger than it takes to wave goodbye to one's next door neighbors as they leave on vacation with a full tank of gas and the proper road maps.

FLIR (Forward Looking Infrared) Sensors—FLIRs, the most important detecting device for the years ahead, have already been fitted into several types of aircraft and are soon to be flying with most American military aircraft. The instrument senses the differences in ground-level thermal radiation and projects them on a screen. According to an Air Force witness before a recent Congressional committee, the results are "hardly distinguishable from a TV picture." Perfect for fighting at night or in poor weather, it is also a handy item to have aboard on the clearest of days to spot camouflaged targets. A major bonus of the FLIR's 24-hour picture is the ability to spot warm objects, which show up as intense white blips—especially neat because so many targets are warm like tank and truck engines, gun barrels and humans. Those with a little experience in the ways of infrared can actually pick out an empty from a full oil storage tank. Besides planes, FLIRs will be showing up on ships, in air defense systems, and in cheap, expendable versions on missiles where they will be used to find and transmit back to a human operator information on targets at night. FLIRs have already been used in combat. In Vietnam they, like so much rough draft equipment tested there, debuted as aids to gunships looking for action along the Ho Chi Minh Trail. They have also been employed by the United States Border Patrol to find drug smugglers.

Grasshopper—This is a new Air Force mine undergoing an advanced development that the late Rube Goldberg would surely have invented had his goal been killing other people. As now envisioned, a number of these 65-pound mines will be distributed from a large dispenser over a target area. Upon hitting the ground each mine will bury itself in the dirt to await passing targets. Its own special Grasshopper logic gives it the ability to distinguish between targets and it will actually be able to activate and deactivate itself as the target moves in and out of sensing range. When the target actually comes close enough to be hit, however, it will pop out of the ground and explode high enough above the ground for maximum damage.

Grasshopper is not alone in combining electronic razzle-dazzle with plain old explosives. MIMS (Multiple Independently Maneuvering Submunition), for instance is a slim bomb about the size and shape of a baseball bat. Each has its own guidance system that locks it onto energy radiated by a vehicle's metal. They are dropped in large quantities from cannisters over target areas where they zoom about like so many dragonflies looking for tanks and armored vehicles.

Less sophisticated but no less devastating is a new class of weaponry called the FAM or "fuel air munition" that accomplishes on purpose what an exploding propane truck does accidentally: level city blocks. The air around the target is filled with an explosive cloud, which is detonated rather than burned. In one configuration now being tested a large cannister of propylene oxide bursts open over a target that is trailed by a high-explosive device about 65 feet behind the cannister. Unlike the Vietnam-era fragmentation weapons, from which under ideal conditions one could conceivably hide, the new FAMs can literally explode around corners and are thus preferred.

IBCS (Integrated Battlefield Control System)—IBCS serves rather nicely to demonstrate that items like those described in this little catalogue are not meant to work alone (although many can) but plug into one another. This particular bit of integration is a major Army program aimed at reducing manpower and increasing combat efficiency by applying automation to battle functions ranging from logistics to psychological tactics. Collectively, it is a big hunk of electronics, which in the words of one of its architects will ". . . integrate the five functions of land combat—mobility, firepower, intelligence, support and command, and control." Major elements of this system now under development include the Tacfire system in which hand-held, digital devices tied to field computer centers will direct firepower; TOS or the Tactical Operations System, which will eventually take on 17 battlefield jobs including keeping track of where friendly and enemy troops are located; and CS3 or the Computer Service Support System, which is a computer system mounted in a van that keeps track of logistics and supplies in combat areas. Tacfire, TOS, CS3, and the rest of this automated shooting match has been described by Army Brigadier General Wilson R. Reed as a whole that ". . . will electronically tie the sensors to the reactive means—the 'beep' to the 'boom' as it were—and leave the soldiers free to do what they do best—think, coordinate, control. The potential seems limitless."

Within the context of IBCS it is important to note that the Army is not just looking for a little computing help, but is attempting some truly major advances in the ways war is fought. One such goal is "first-round targeting capability" which means creating a system that will detect the first round of incoming enemy artillery and, by computing its trajectory, pinpoint the location of the gun that fired it—instantaneously! Several highly-promising approaches have been developed to achieve this goal including a 3-D radar system from the Hughes Aircraft Company.

Laser Weapons—Between 1965 and 1968 several hundred missions were flown against a heavily defended bridge—dubbed the Dragon's Jaw by US airmen—at Thanh Hoa on the railroad line running south of Hanoi. By 1968, the bridge not only remained in near-mint condition, but the United States had squandered ten planes and as many crews on the target. When

President Nixon ordered a resumption of bombing above the 17th parallel in March 1972, the bridge was again on the high priority target list. On March 13 several Air Force F-4Ds went into the area for a first shot at the bridge and came out reporting that it was in the water, a feat accomplished without the loss of a single plane.

The Dragon's Jaw affair is simply the most commonly cited of many such incidents that illustrate the devastating accuracy of guided or "smart" bombs, which had quietly crept into the war on an experimental basis in early 1971 and were a major factor a year later. To hear the military talk, some of these incidents described a kind of precision long dreamed of but hardly expected before the year 2000.* For instance, Colonel Richard D. Hilton, writing in *Army* magazine, describes one such case in the spring of 1972:

> After several weeks of successful strikes the Organization of the Joint Chiefs of Staff (OJCS) targeted the Lang Chi hydroelectric generators northwest of Hanoi. The difficulty of this target lay in the fact that the generators were located only a few feet from a dam which held back a lake about three miles wide and ten miles long. If the dam were ruptured during the strikes on the generators a great wall of water would flood Hanoi and the Red River basin. Flooding the basin would be politically unacceptable, but the generators were significant to the North Vietnamese war effort and should be put out of commission. The OJCS was confident that our crews could destroy the generators without hitting the dam. Again we succeeded without the loss of a strike aircraft.

Such successes caused the 7th Air Force in Saigon to officially conclude that the North Vietnamese suffered more damage to key installations in the first 60 days of "smart" bombing in Nixon's

---

* Apparently, the military could have had this Space Age marvel a bit earlier. *Science* magazine reported in 1972 that the technology was ready to go in 1967 but those who had developed the "smart" bomb could find no takers.

"Linebacker" operation than had been inflicted in the four years of Lyndon Johnson's "Rolling Thunder" bombing operation against the North. Significantly, *Aviation Week and Space Technology*, arbiter of all that flies, was quick to sum it all up by concluding that the new bombs ". . . are destroying with surgical precision targets that previously were spattered by large quantities of bombs that inflicted only minor and easily repairable damage."

Besides rendering dumb into smart, there was added importance in this turn of technological events. Though all smart bombs are not laser-guided (some are TV-guided), it was of major significance that the laser had come out of the lab and into the modern arsenal.

Since 1972—the Stone Age of lasers, say today's experts, who add that we are now at the Model-T stage—a host of new applications and refinements have been actively sought as part of a multi-million dollar (about $300 million for 1975) effort involving all the services. As one might expect, there are the smarter and more sophisticated second generation laser-guided bombs like the 2,000-pound Pave Storm, which carries 750 smaller bombs making it nearly three times larger than any earlier cluster bomb.

Taking this same technology to another area, there is the Army's cannon-launched guided projectile (CLGP) or "smart" shell. It is now in advanced development and the Army claims it is scoring six direct hits for every seven pushes of the button. A man near the target uses his laser designator—which either looks like a very fat rifle or a very fat pistol depending on the model—to mark the point of impact and then the shell, fired from as far away as ten miles, homes in on the beam. Others are working on "smart" missiles (not exactly dumb to begin with) as part of the Beam Rider program, and it is well within the reach of technology to field a system in which a man fingers a target with his beam and a passing plane "loans" him a smart bomb to zap it. It appears that the "smart" technology will soon reach down to the level of just about every foot soldier. *Electronics* magazine quoted a military official who talks about "an ultracheap [laser designator] device that they can give to every man—just like a canteen."

Meanwhile, lasers are working their way into all sorts of other military applications. The Navy, among others, is working on a laser voice communications system, several laser intrusion detection systems have been developed (with much the same effect as the electric eye on the supermarket door but able to work over much longer distances), and the Air Force is developing on a laser, satellite communications system that will be powered by the sun.

There are others, but none is more intriguing than the "death ray" application first put to use by the likes of Flash Gordon and Buck Rogers in their scrapes with the forces of evil. Although few efforts are so heavily wrapped in secrecy, enough is known to conclude that high energy lasers loom very large in the military scheme of things. One group that specializes in finding out about once and future military markets, DMS Incorporated of Old Greenwich, Connecticut, predicted in 1974 that a death ray (or what the Army prefers to term "an instantaneous destruction beam") will join the nation's weapons collection and that eventually just about every airplane, tank, and ship will carry at least one device "capable of searching out and destroying enemy forces with beams of light millions of times brighter than the sun."

Now in development are offensive lasers to be used against targets like aircraft and tanks as well as defensive ones that would come into play in zapping ballistic missiles from the ground and in voiding surface to air missiles from a bomber. Even as of this writing, these applications do not seem that far away to anyone keeping up with laser-related tidbits that appear on the pages of the military and electronics magazines. At the end of 1974, *Aerospace Daily* reported that lasers ". . . have been used to shoot down airborne targets, described as resembling RPVs," and a few months later *Electronics* told of a new laser able to "burn through heavy stainless nickel steel at range."

SIAM (Self-Initiated Antiaircraft Munition)—Perhaps the last word in automated death is the sensor that decides who will die without even the courtesy of a human rubber-stamp OK. (Is it a purely romantic and outmoded notion to think that there is something especially futile and grotesque about dying just because your body or the vehicle you are riding in creates the right blip to trigger the ganglia of an electronic device?)

All that has been made public about this system is a few lines in the written ARPA budget request for fiscal year 1975, but from that it would appear that it is a sensor which is fired into an area where it remains dormant until a "target" gives off the right combination of signals, at which time it fires a distant missile and brings it down on the target, of which it has been keeping track. Even though a system that sophisticated will cost a lot, Congress did not once question it during the 1976 appropriation and authorization process, and ARPA never mentioned it again.

Space Lasers—Since the Second World War one of the most reliable places to look for clues as to what is going to appear on future military want lists is to examine the advanced inquiries by the RAND Corporation, the Santa Monica think tank that has done most of its work for the Air Force since it was founded by that service in 1946. The 1973–1974 edition of *RAND Annual Report* takes a hard look at spaceborne laser systems, which, it adds editorially, could be as important to the military world of the 1990s as radar was after the Second World War. "We are assuming the future capabilities of instruments in surveillance navigation, communication, and meteorology satellites," says the report, "and are evaluating their potentially combined impact on strategic bomber and missile forces."

Survsatcom (Survivable Satellite Communications)—A space-borne system that will be in operation by the 1980s, which will allow the president, Joint Chiefs, and other well-placed, aging members of the first television generation to get live TV pictures from virtually any corner of the world. It is the most sophisticated of several electronic battlefield components that will make war a TV spectator sport replete with provisions for slow motion replays to verify smart bomb hits, subtle course changes made by cruise missiles, and the like.

When operating in conjunction with the right weapons, Survsatcom will give future commanders-in-chief godlike sensations and abilities not even hinted at when kings were divine. For example, an advanced form of the crude meteorological warfare pioneered in Vietnam (when the US often succeeded in making it rain on the Ho Chi Minh Trail) might not only allow a future president to order up a typhoon, tornado, or just a bad day for flying, but also allow him to watch it all in color from a cozy armchair in an Oval Office halfway around the world.

For all their diversity, the items in this sampling of the new hardware going on line or in the pipeline are remarkably similar on one key point: thanks to the latest technology they are all able to promise more death and destruction on the "other" side for fewer men risked on the side of electronics.

One case speaks for many by showing how dramatically the equation on the battlefield can change with just one major improvement. In the spring of 1975 Army Assistant Secretary Norman R. Augustine made this rather stunning accounting for the aforementioned cannon-launched guided projectile (CLGP):

This development promises to give to artillery . . . for the first time in history, the capability to efficiently attack fixed and moving hard point targets with indirect fire. The saving in people this economy of firepower could entail will cascade itself all the way back through the support system . . . the savings achievable in the logistic pipeline alone amount to about five transportation companies and two ammunition companies, or about 1,200 spaces, [read people] when fighting a NATO war.

Yet even after being given such a hard-nosed rationale as making war less labor intensive, one must still concede that these will be spectacular items if they work—dynamic bits of American technological derring-do, which if they were not used to kill would provide a great source of entertainment with all their blipping, zooming, and zapping. Rather than end with the brief introduction to some of them just concluded, it seems appropriate to go one step further and single one out for a more detailed look, to gain a better appreciation and feel for what is being wrought. One that begs for such detail is a development that one can easily argue may be the most revolutionary of them all, the Remotely Piloted Vehicle.

EIGHT

Robot Air Force

RPVs Don't Chicken Out.

—Motto used by backers of unmanned aircraft.

PLANES WITHOUT PILOTS

Like a golfer selecting a club from his bag, the military pilot of the 1980s will be able to select the plane best suited for the martial drive, chip shot, or putt he is about to make. If all goes according to plan, his specific choices will include:

—A small but lethal "Kamikaze" to be used as an explosive ram against the enemy plane, ship, munitions depot, or other target of his choice. A one-way, hence cheap, instrument which may be electric powered.

—A sleek, lightweight model employing a TV camera to locate a target and a laser designator to mark and illuminate it. Moments after the laser has spotted the target a missile or bomb is dispatched to home in on its beam and destroy the target.

—A truly tiny plane, not any bigger than the kind that model airplane enthusiasts use, which is electronically configured so that it is able to portray itself on a radar screen as a transport, bomber, or fighter. This little item comes in handy as a decoy used to flush out enemy fighters and surface-to-air missiles.

178

—A plane that is virtually invisible to radar, infrared detection, and, until the last moment, the naked eye. Because it is also silent it is helpful if surprise or secrecy is desired.

As a class these planes are known as remotely piloted vehicles, or more commonly RPVs, and those just described are now in various stages of development. As promised in their name, the one thing they all have in common is that the pilot in charge is not in the plane but is running it by proxy from a ground station or mother ship operating in a safe zone. By means of small, lightweight TV cameras and other sensors carried by the RPVs, the pilot is able to experience the thrill of combat and the sense of danger without the threat of death, injury, or imprisonment as a POW. It is the U-2 without the "you" in it, the sport of the dogfight without its nasty, charred human remains—at least for the side with the RPVs—and the all-out thrill of a screaming Kamikaze strike without even getting your hair mussed.

For those who might find controlling *just one* of these birds too tame, work is now underway that will allow one human to fly a brace of up to 20 of them at one time. Moreover, the pilot of the future will not even need to leave home to wage a foreign war. "With foreign technology being what it is," says George Weiss of Boeing's Washington Office, "there should be no reason why a man won't be able to sit in the basement of the Pentagon and engage in combat in Europe or Asia through a satellite link." In all, an odd prospect: Air combat conducted by men and women who commute to their stationary cockpits for eight-hour stints from their homes in Arlington and Alexandria.

And while the term RPV has yet to enter the realm of household word for civilian America, it can be said without hesitation that these three letters represent the hottest, most talked about single new idea to come to the forefront of the military consciousness in the mid-1970s. Whatever the RPV concept lacks in terms of dollars now pumped into it—about $150 million per year and rising as of 1975—is made up for in enthusiasm. A recent

Army statement on that branch's development program said it may lead to ". . . what may prove to be one of the Army's greatest assets." Nobody less than Air Force Secretary John McLucas is that service's prime spokesman for the RPV. He has termed himself one of the nation's ". . . strongest proponents of RPVs," and predicted that they would become "a significant force" in the future Air Force inventory. On March 1, 1975, the Air Force created a RPV "Super" System Program Office at Wright-Patterson Air Force Base, which is their way of saying they are very, very serious about the idea. *Air Force* magazine said the RPV ". . . may be the closest thing to a panacea the aerospace age has yet created," while *Seapower* magazine predicted that unmanned planes could ". . . revolutionize naval air power as dramatically as nuclear power has already revolutionized the surface and subsurface Navy." Meanwhile, a special organization, the National Association for RPVs, has recently been formed to boost the idea and the product. It should not have a difficult time finding members as more than a dozen major aerospace companies have hung out their RPV shingles to help attract a piece of the billion-dollar-a-year market envisioned by 1980.

The RPV has an interesting lineage stemming most directly from the target drones, robot vehicles used rather routinely over the last 25 years to test and train combat pilots, missilemen, and antiaircraft gunners. The important difference between the RPV and its more simple-minded first cousin, the drone, is that the latter is a preprogrammed automaton given commands in advance of flight, while the RPV is subject to human control during flight. The difference is much the same as that which exists between a paper airplane, programmed after a fashion by the arm that throws it, and a kite that is under human control through its string, which is akin to the electronic control the person on the ground has over the RPV. However, as the differences between the drone and RPV get very fine at times—is a drone subject to human correction an RPV?—and because the term RPV has begun to be applied widely for sophisticated drones as well, the terms have merged into one with RPV the surviving partner in the merger.

The drone/RPV idea actually goes back to the technology of the First World War. The grandparents of today's unmanned vehicles were the Kettering "Bug" and Sperry "Aerial Torpedo" used in 1917 and 1918. They were winged carts on wheels with engines that somehow managed to lift them into the air after a fast start on a pair of rails. Though they flew, they left much to be desired in terms of sophistication and were not useful as an accurate, winged bomb. The urge to launch manless planes was abandoned for the moment.

More successful, however, was the effort that lasted from 1928 to 1932 in which a Curtis "Robin" aircraft was turned into a working drone. Then, in the late 1930s there was a rush of military interest in remotely controlled vehicles, which led to a raft of "special weapons" including a second "Bug," essentially a surface-to-surface "buzz" bomb, and the "Bat," a radio-controlled glide bomb. Out of this pack came the first truly usable weapon: the crude but lethal GB-1, which was a 2,000-pound bomb with plywood wings and rudders and a radio-control package. These were dropped from B-17s and visually guided by bombardiers to their target. In 1943, 108 GB-1s were dropped on Cologne causing heavy damage. For propaganda reasons (perhaps mixed with a genuine inability to comprehend what had happened) the Germans officially reported that they were able to turn back the bombers before any bombs were dropped. Their report continued, "The accompanying fighter cover, however, composed of small exceedingly fast twin-tailed aircraft, came over the city at low altitude in a strafing attack. So good were the defenses that every single fighter was shot down; much damage was done by these falling aircraft, all of which exploded violently." Later in the war came the GB-4 "Robin," the first television-guided weapon.

Certainly the most tragic and fascinating moment in the early story of airborne robots came about late in the war in the form of a top secret English-based effort known as Project Aphrodite, which had as its goal the destruction of German rocket research and launching sites concealed in caves and heavily fortified bunkers. The urgency of the project was further intensified by dark suspicions on the part of American intelligence that the Nazis were preparing rockets for an attack on New York City. The plan was to take war-weary B-17 and B-24 bombers, strip them of all but the most essential equipment, and cram them full of high explosives—as it turned out, the most powerful flown in war to that time. Live crews were to get the planes in the air and out over the Channel at which point they would bail out and a manned mother ship would take control. The highly explosive bomber could presumably zero into the mouths of the caves and large bunkers by the combination of a TV in the tip of the robot, and the radio control system.

Aphrodite was a complete failure. A number of planes did not even get near their targets and those that did somehow managed to miss their mark at the last moment. The financial cost was high and a number of pilots and crewmen died during the effort, including young Joseph Kennedy, Jr., who with a crewman was scattered across the British countryside when his B-17 exploded before they were to bail out. The details of the young Kennedy's death were officially kept secret for years, and it was not until his brother became president that the full circumstances even became known to the family.* The irony was that those priority targets that Aphrodite was unable to harm had been abandoned before the project started, and when Allied foot soldiers entered them they found only rubble, roaches, and rats.

---

* In his 1970 book, *Aphrodite: Desperate Mission,* Jack Olsen not only made the story of Aphrodite public and clear for the first time but added a chilling footnote to the tragic tale. The day that John F. Kennedy chose to meet with the family of the young Texan who had died with his brother was the day that he was killed in Dallas.

Despite that spectacular failure, the military was not giving up. After the war, the concepts at play in Aphrodite, the German, gasoline-burning V-1, and the far more sophisticated V-2 ballistic rocket led to the immediate acceleration of American plans to develop guided missiles. But missiles were one thing and winged drones another, and a special Pilotless Aircraft Branch of the Air Force came into being in late 1946 to develop three types of drones for use as training targets. Of the three, the jet Q-2 was the most ambitious, and also the most important in that it became the father of a class of drones built by the Ryan Aeronautical Company (now Teledyne-Ryan), which has given that company undisputed leadership in the field. The Q-2 developed into more than 20 distinct models each with its own name and number given by the service that commissioned them. Ryan has been calling all of them its Firebees.

Since Ryan got its first contract more than 4,000 Firebees have been sold to the three services and the drones have performed many impressive and diverse tasks. They have flown at levels from 50 to 60,000 feet, moved at speeds from 200 to 500 knots, and stayed aloft for periods of up to 2 hours at a clip. Virtually every antiaircraft system the nation has developed has had to prove its worth by downing a batch of elusive Firebees (or targets towed by Firebees). Devices have been created to make the small Firebee show up on radar as a bomber and modifications have been made in some that have enabled them to make the dives and turns that real pilots "fighting" them can make. Recently a special Firebee II has been created for the Navy that is capable of speeds in excess of 1,000 miles per hour.

Ryan, however, has been far from alone in finding ways to use planes without pilots. In the mid-1950s, for example, Sperry rigged an F-80 fighter so that it could be flown automatically to fetch radioactive atmospheric samples from recent nuclear blast areas —hardly the kind of mission that men stand in line to volunteer for. However, despite such applications, the unmanned airplane was almost entirely regarded as a target for training pilots and missilemen through the late 1960s.

AGE OF THE RPV

By 1970 enough key people in the military establishment were beginning to think that there was more promise to the drone than as an ever more sophisticated moving target, because the technology was available that would allow them to be piloted from the ground. This caused the Air Force and its favorite think tank, the RAND Corporation, to sit down for a symposium on the future possibilities of remotely piloted vehicles. After that meeting and some follow-up studies, a consensus emerged among the military planners: there was, indeed, considerable promise in the RPV for a variety of military applications, which had been made possible through a decade of rapid advances in electronic technology.

While RAND helped pave the way for the dawning of the age of the RPV, the truly dramatic turn in the way the military regards robot planes has come about through a quick succession of events, realizations, and demonstrations. First and most telling are the remarkable feats that the unmanned machines have performed to the humiliation of manned systems. The most dramatic to come to light was an aerial "dogfight" staged in early 1971 over the Pacific Test Range, which pitted a manned Navy F-4 Phantom against a Ryan Firebee outfitted with a remote flight control system, making it a true RPV. The unmanned fighter, maneuvered by a man on the ground, not only averted two air-to-air missile assaults, but scored several simulated "hits" on the F-4, which, incidentally, is the nation's finest fighter plane. The Firebee executed turns so radical—and impossible for the F-4 and even the forthcoming highly touted F-15—that it was able to reverse direction in only twenty seconds, a fraction of the time taken by a manned plane because a man can only take so much gravitational pressure. Nor was that the only experiment in which the formerly hunted became a successful hunter. In 1972 a supersonic Firebee II penetrated the missile defenses of the Navy destroyer *Wainwright* and scored a simulated direct hit.

Second, while the impact of these simulated victories was absorbed by the Pentagon, a pair of realizations regarding men and planes became painfully evident. Human pilots all of a sudden began to look very vulnerable. About 90 percent of the American POWs in Southeast Asia were downed pilots and airmen, and a total of 5,000 Americans died in hostile and nonhostile aircraft incidents in that war in which there was hardly major opposition from the North Vietnamese Air Force. The lesson was taught elsewhere too. Israel watched many of its best aviators fall to Arab missiles and guns in the early days of the fourth Arab-Israeli conflict. Many of these losses came in what amounted to situations in which the Israeli pilots were testing Arab air defenses, a job that should have been done by unmanned decoys.

That manned aircraft are highly vulnerable is not a discovery —the United States lost 40,000 aircraft and twice as many pilots and crewmen during the Second World War—but the results of conflict in Southeast Asia and the Middle East still came as a shock. Those who believed that the latest high-performance aircraft would beat the odds were wrong. What is more, the future appeared even bleaker. As the RAND Corporation's William B. Graham wrote in *Astronautics and Aeronautics*, "Anti-aircraft defenses will get tougher and tougher as far into the future as anyone can foresee."

Just as it became obvious that the RPV could reduce human waste, it also became obvious that it could reduce fiscal waste. While the Vietnam experience underscored the human costs of manned aircraft, spiraling defense costs and the runaway inflation of the early 1970s brought the financial picture into sharp focus. A recent study for the Air Force, again by the RAND Corporation, determined that the costs of manned aircraft are going up at such a rate that if the Air Force's budget were to remain constant in the face of rising costs, they could only afford a dozen planes by the year 2000 and only one in 2020.

Because it does not have to support a human crew the RPV can not only be smaller, but can leave out all those highly expensive elements needed to keep men alive—oxygen systems, ejector seats, heavy armor plate, fire detection systems, communications gear, and much more. Without men to support, all sorts of economies are possible including the use of such materials as fiberglass, plastic foam, fabric, and even cardboard. As many have pointed out quite seriously, once you get humans out of the plane you can start borrowing ideas from the realm of the model aircraft hobbyist. For these reasons the generally accepted rule of thumb is that the cost of an RPV versus a manned craft with the same function works out to be twenty to thirty times cheaper. This ratio, which is for reusable RPVs, jumps to hundreds of times cheaper when you talk about bare-bones one-way RPVs for highly dangerous or suicidal missions.

While the dollars and cents economies of the planes themselves are tremendous there are also more savings promised in terms of support costs, pilot costs, and, because they are harder to hit, planes lost in combat. Today the military states that it costs about $500,000 to train a pilot to the point that he is ready to fight. The figure is an interesting one because the military now estimates that $500,000 will be the top price for the most sophisticated RPV of the 1980s while simpler models will cost as little as $10,000.

As the human and dollar advantages of the RPV loom larger and larger in the minds of post-Vietnam era military planners, a less obvious but just as appealing point for the RPV has come to light. The RPV promises to allow the military to do what it has been unable to do for at least a decade: mount a highly visible weapons development effort that will impress the Congress and the public alike because it is replacing something expensive with something *truly inexpensive*.* Although the economy of the RPV is hardly noticeable in terms of the total expenses of the automated battlefield, the bottom-line results from the RPV are already regarded as a major public relations coup for the military in inflationary times. The novelty of a cheap system has occasioned several widely circulated and intentionally tongue-in-cheek "bits" about the prospects. One has it that the only way for existing aerospace companies to do anything cheap will be to set up a special plant away from the head office staffed with engineers with no experience working on military hardware. Another is that the RPV work will have to be taken away from the aerospace industry and given to one that has the needed imagination and skill to keep costs under control: namely, the toy industry.

The final factor in the quick turn to the RPV as a major element in the upcoming American arsenal has been the fact that it has proven itself in real combat situations—something that has attracted scant attention outside military circles. Air Force sources casually admit that they were used as early as 1962 for reconnaissance over Cuba, and a year later Ryan 147 drones were pressed into service for low-level spy missions over North Vietnam, Laos, and the People's Republic of China. Launched by C-130 "mother" ships, these sleek, black, unmarked craft were first brought out of the shadows when the Chinese claimed to have brought one down on November 15, 1964. The United States refused to admit to this or later allegations by the Chinese about American robots in their skies. In early 1965, when the Chinese were saying that they had bagged a total of eight, three moderately damaged examples were put on public view at the Chinese People's Revolutionary Museum in Peking and pictures were released of the display. Even so, the "no comments" from the

---

* A 1972 RAND Corporation paper cites one small example: high velocity aerial targets for the Army made from the same heavy cardboard tubing used to roll carpet.

State Department, CIA, and Pentagon continued for some time, but nobody looking at the evidence could seriously doubt that the US had given the lion's share of its close-in surveillance work in Asia to the Ryan drones.

With the Air Force now admitting that some 3,000 unmanned missions were flown during America's period of active involvement in Southeast Asia, the record of the robot spies is coming out and it is most dramatic. The attrition rate for the planes was less than four percent (including one shot down by a Navy interceptor, which had mistaken it for a hostile MIG-21) because they were routinely recovered in mid-air when helicopters snagged them by the parachutes they spewed out at mission's end. About 85 percent of the photos taken to assess bomb damage during the period were brought home by these automated craft. Often unknown to both those who looked at them and those that published them, many of the aerial views of North Vietnam that appeared in the American press were taken by the drones.

Needless to say, not one American life was lost, nor were there any Francis Gary Powers types to bring to trial, fuss over, and parade about for propaganda reasons. Firebees were also assuming the jobs of waterborne electronic intelligence gathering vessels. One only has to recall the *Liberty* and *Pueblo* disasters to see that this was a highly important development. In terms of actual performance, in at least one case the Ryan sea craft was able to bring home photos of an area in North Vietnam that two unmanned planes had been unable to get.

Meanwhile there were other Vietnam-era applications. One group, which was quickly dubbed "The Bullshit Bombers," was used to dispense American propaganda leaflets around Hanoi and other population centers. One specific example occurred on Christmas Day 1969 when leaflets containing President Nixon's picture and a plea for peace were dropped. Others were used as electronic listening devices, and automated QU-22B Beech aircraft were used to pick up and relay sensor signals broadcast from the Ho Chi Minh Trail during Operation Igloo White. Still another application, as a dispenser for radar-befouling chaff, was developed but such use was severely limited because there were not enough C-130 mother ships to go around.

The RPV has also had its combat debut in the Middle East. Learning a lesson from earlier losses, during the Yom Kippur War the Israelis used a number of Northrop Chukar drones as decoys on which to get the Arabs to expend surface-to-air missiles as manned planes slipped in behind them. It is also no secret that the Israelis have used and continue to use Ryan-built craft for photo reconnaissance missions and have been highly pleased with them. Furthermore, there is little question that the Israelis have the ability to build their own model RPV and some have speculated that they are now developing one of their own. In short, there are compelling reasons for the military's interest in RPVs.

THE WILD, BLUE, REMOTE-CONTROLLED YONDER

All of this brings us to the present and the active motion on the part of all three services and the Department of Defense as a whole to come up with a raft of vehicle types, applications packages, and technological refinements. The list of developments that have actually begun or are about to is long; but descriptions of the highlights and major trends should serve to give a good picture of what is going on. Much of the information was given to me in a detailed briefing by the knowledgeable James P. Morgan, assistant director of the RPV System Program Office at Wright-Patterson Air Force Base.

Considerable hope, attention, and money is being expended on a sleek RPV with a 90-foot wingspan called Compass Cope that, according to Morgan, looks as if it will become the nation's primary high-altitude spy plane for the late 1970s and 1980s.

Under Air Force sponsorship, Ryan and Boeing have produced prototype versions of the fiberglass plane, which has already flaunted abilities unmatched by manned craft. The Ryan version of this trim, gliderlike plane has flown for over 24 hours without refueling, which is much longer than any manned plane in the Air Force stable can fly. That plus its ability to cruise at altitudes above 60,000 feet will contribute to its role as an intelligence gathering platform that loiters at altitudes far above the weather.

While Compass Cope and most other RPVs are meant to return from their missions to fly another day, the Air Force is also developing a nonreturnable, one way vehicle called TEDS (short for Tactical Expendable Drone System). These relatively cheap RPVs would be used to confuse, harass, and, when armed with a small warhead, attack an enemy. One way they could be used is in a dummy strike force, piloted and electronically configured to look like a full-fledged manned bombing strike thereby saturating and confusing the enemy radar and causing the enemy to commit missiles and planes . . . or they could be used to flood an area with jamming devices. Morgan says, "If you could get a lot of them to the right place in a hurry, like Europe, you could accomplish a lot with just a few planes with blue suits in them." He adds, "There are still some questions to be answered, but I think we'll be going into full-scale development and production." One of those questions is how cheap is relatively cheap? Best guess: under $10,000.

Another program that the Air Force feels shows great promise is the MMMRPV (for Modular, Multi-Mission RPV), a versatile jack-of-all-trades unit that can easily be converted to electronic warfare, strike or reconnaissance uses. This renaissance RPV will carry a wide variety of sensors and weapons. A simple "interim" MMMRPV is now being readied by the Air Force, and an advanced version is expected to debut in the 1980s.

Finally, there are the mini-RPVs that bid to be the most intriguing of the breed. Besides their weight and size—less than

200 pounds and a wingspan of less than 12 feet—the mini's outstanding characteristic is that its technology is essentially a scaled-up version of that of the model airplane rather than a scaled-down version of manned aircraft technology. In fact, Maynard Hill of the Johns Hopkins Applied Physics Laboratory is one of several people whose hobby has crossed the line to become research of interest to the Department of Defense—in his case the Advanced Research Projects Agency. Hill, who has worked with model planes since he was a boy and who holds thirteen international records in that field, has used a model plane to come up with an inexpensive electrostatic autopilot, which may find wide use as an RPV stabilization system.

While the Air Force clearly dominates the larger RPVs, the Army and Navy are big sponsors of the mini-RPV. The major Navy effort began in 1974 as an exploratory program called STAR (Ship Tactical Airborne RPV), which ultimately aimed at producing a plane of less than 100 pounds that can be operated by men with a minimum of training from the decks of ships. This vehicle will be cheap, crude (it will probably be recovered in a net), and make its mark as a forward target locating and designating device. It may also see service as a medium for carrying messages between ships and as an electronic data relay point.

The major Army efforts, which also interest the other services, are the Kamikaze (its official name) and RPAODS (for Remotely Piloted Aerial Observation/Designation System). The Kamikaze effort thus far points to an ultimate product weighing under 50 pounds without payload, which will be piloted with the help of a tiny TV camera and will be sufficiently accurate to hit without trouble a target the size of a tank. RPAODS is one of several programs aimed at getting the RPV to find a target, and, like a pointer-dog, keep a bead on it with its laser nose until a laser-guided bomb or missile comes in from elsewhere to home in on the target. The ground-based pilot in this system has two planes, a daytime version that allows him to look for the target with a TV camera (replete with zoom lens), and a night version with an infrared sensor. One plane now bidding to be RPAODS workhorse is Philco-Ford's Praeire II (pronounced pray-ere, it comes from the Latin meaning "leading soldier"), which loiters near its target for relatively long periods of time.

If the mini-RPVs sound a bit science fictionlike in the abstract, they tend to reinforce that image in the flesh. For instance, the mini-RPV that was unveiled by Teledyne-Ryan in late 1974 is a flying delta wing with a rounded nose, which looks like one of those tricornered apple turnovers. This flying pastry look is only slightly countered by two tiny fins and a small, rear-mounted prop. Since it weighs less than 150 pounds fully fueled and can be moved around by two people of moderate strength, it cuts an odd image as a serious contender for taking on a variety of future military missions.

Compass Cope, TEDS, MMMRPV, STAR, the Kamikaze, and RPAODS are only part of the future robot air force now taking shape, but are enough to show that that force will be a diverse and multifunctioned mix. Not all of the work in this field is aimed at one plane or program but it is also applied to the technology of RPVs in general. Two high priority goals for RPVs as a class are to make them as close to unjammable as possible and to boost the number that one operator can fly at one time, which is now only four.

Then, somewhat further down the road, there are these very real RPV possibilities:

The Civilian RPV—Thus far it has been mainly talk and it should remain so until more is learned about them, but it would appear that serious consideration will be given to the use of RPVs for civilian jobs. The one most commonly mentioned is as an instrument to spot forest fires, but other ideas ranging from crime surveillance to search planes for lost ships and peopled aircraft have been mentioned. One of the most interesting ideas in this area was put forth in an article in *Astronautics and Aeronautics* by three men from Developmental Sciences Incorporated who have come up with the idea of the Remotely Piloted Mini-Blimp (RPMB), a small nonrigid airship employing emerging RPV technology. The authors argue that there are a host of urban jobs for these little blimps equipped with RPV controls and light, cheap TV cameras, including pollution measurement and monitoring, and automobile traffic reporting.

The Remote Boat—The V in RPV stands for *vehicle,* which of course does not just mean aircraft, and it should come as no surprise that thought has been given to boat RPVs. To date the Navy has been principally interested in the RPV as an airborne weapon but the technological jump to boats could be quite simple. James D. Hessman, editor in chief of *Seapower,* has suggested in his magazine, "Radio controlled from air, sea or shore, small boat RPVs, especially constructed to make them almost invisible to radar, could dart out from protective shorelines to make sudden strikes against enemy naval and merchant shipping. San Diego Aircraft Engineering Incorporated (Sandaire) has proposed two offensive RPV weapons to be built from existing hardware: a 28-foot "deep V" hulled boat able to carry 1,000 pounds of explosives at 45 knots, and a larger, surface riding boat able to attack at 40 knots with a two-ton payload. The company says both of these attack craft could be dropped into combat areas by helicopter.

The "Invisible" RPV—One RPV aspect that, according to a variety of military sources, will come in for increasing R&D attention is minimizing its observable characteristics. Envisioned here is an RPV so small that it is essentially invisible to radar, so quiet that it cannot be heard, so small and well camouflaged as to be hard to spot with the naked eye, and so well shrouded that it gives off no infrared signal. Little money has yet to be appropriated for this effort, but there is no doubt that it appeals to the military, which should be looking for funds to pay for squadrons

of practically silent and invisible RPVs. A typical attitude is that
of David R. Heebner, deputy director of defense research and
engineering, who views the reduction of RPV observables as an
exciting and important course to pursue.

Beyond these, there are doubtless some fanciful and bizarre
variations on the theme now either under investigation or
development that are hidden from view for the simple reason that
a sizable amount of this work is classified (although it may not be
as much as it was in 1971 when Teledyne-Ryan said that 60
percent of its RPV work was either officially classified or
sensitive). The more astonishing variations will come from the
Advanced Research Projects Agency (ARPA), which is known to
be looking into a solar-powered, high-altitude, long-endurance
RPV as well as an exceedingly cheap harassment vehicle costing
less than $1,000 a copy in quantities of 5,000 or more.

Of course, a disclaimer must be made here to the effect that the
RPV cannot entirely replace the manned aircraft in the foreseeable future if for no other reason than that of maintaining the
morale of Air Force officers who are also pilots. However, all signs
point to RPVs coming in for a greater and greater piece of the
action. The record of unmanned reconnaissance flights in Southeast Asia makes it inconceivable that Americans will ever again
routinely fly that kind of mission just as none will presumably fly
into the jaws-of-death type situation in which enemy air defenses
are tested. Aside from American lives saved the further rationale
is hard to miss. As *Aviation Week* put it so concisely when it said a
few years back, ". . . the impending low-profile military posture
of the United States will impose greater demands on techniques
involving low human risk, minimal expense and little reliance on
foreign offshore military bases"—fitting for the RPV as well as the
larger automated concept it is part of and growing with.

NINE

The Electronic Battlefield— Buy Now, Think Later!

[There is already] growing dependence of arms systems on complex and rapid computer-controlled response and consequent erosion of the control of political leaders over final decisions.

In the extreme this could lead to systems which would be triggered on warning of attack, thereby placing the fate of the superpowers and the world entirely in hands of radars and other sensors, and the computers and technicians which control and interpret them.

—From the report on New Technology and the Arms Race *prepared by 26 weapons experts at Racine, Wisconsin, June 1970.*

I became fascinated with the electronic battlefield when I first began picking up information on parts of it while working as a writer for *Electronics* magazine in Washington in the late 1960s. I was awed and angered. My awe was for the technological virtuosity involved, the challenge of mounting it, and the combination of Dr. Strangelove and Buck Rogers—things that go zap in the night and all that. The anger focused on the use to which it was being put as a death-dealing instrument in Southeast Asia

195

and, on a more general level, the slick, casual kind of war of the future in which killing would be programmed like a department store billing system.

My fascination has continued, but, during the intervening years as a self-appointed lay expert, my attitude towards the electronic battlefield has become less impressionistic (although awe and anger still feed my interest) and more centered on a set of bothersome, unanswered questions and specific objections.

Several quick points must be made before moving onto these critical areas. The first is that this criticism is not meant to be addressed exclusively to the United States, but to all similar developments taking place within the technologically advanced community of nations, capitalist and communist.* However, the clear American lead in electronic battlefield technology and my interest in the priorities of my nation dictate using the US as the prime example in all of the questions raised. Second, it should in no way be presumed that by questioning the electronic battlefield I do not recognize that elements of it might be important in saving American lives when the nation is at war. In a strictly defensive situation, for instance, it is hard to imagine anything more helpful than a set of sensors that record enemy actions without ordering scouts into hostile areas. After the appearance of a magazine article I wrote on the subject of the electronic battlefield in which I raised a few of the above questions, I got a letter from a man who claimed that by questioning the system I did not allow for the saving of American lives and that I must therefore consider them

---

* Information on Soviet advances in electronic battlefield technology is difficult to come by and dished out on a selective basis by American sources. More than a dozen experts I interviewed refused to tell me anything about Soviet work on unattended ground sensors because the answer was sensitive. On the other hand, in making its case for "cruise" missiles the military has made detailed public presentations on Soviet strength in that area. From what I have been able to piece together, the Soviet Union is pursuing some of the same things the US is but clearly not all of them. Also, one can, I have been told by experts, presume that the USSR is working on countermeasures to most elements of the American electronic battlefield.

to be "highly expendable." Nothing could be further from the truth. Underlying most of these questions is the premise that the application of electronic war invites us to devalue human life because of its promise of easy, push-button killing. This is liable to have nothing to do with saving American lives but with cutting down the maximum number on the other side. Also, one must ask, if a nation puts a very low value on foreign life, how much longer will it be until it begins to lower the value of its own citizens?

It should also be mentioned that there are a limited but certain number of applications that would seem to prevent rather than to foster hostilities. Using sensors as an example, several authorities in the world of arms control have suggested the use of sensors to monitor nuclear test bans, both above and below ground, in the United States and USSR. As a method for border surveillance the sensor would seem to be as good a way as any of keeping track of those who might cross your border and do you harm. It might be just the thing to make a nation less liable to invade for fear of immediate detection. But even an application like that can be threatening if installed without control. One group that has looked closely at the potential of sensors in the wars of the future is the Stockholm Peace Research Institute (SIPRI), which in a recent report warned that there is a great danger in adding an automatic weapons launching capacity to the sensor in such a border-watching situation, particularly in peacetime, "as a warhead released automatically and erroneously by a computer might hit foreign territory or even foreign border troops, with very grave consequences."

The prime case in point illustrating the potentially peaceful deployment of sensors is of course the proposed "Kissinger Line" of American equipment and technicians to be stationed between Arab and Israeli troops in the Sinai as part of a Sinai peace accord. As of early 1976 no details on the equipment to be installed had been made public and about all the State Department would say about it was that it would contain the latest in American electronic listening equipment and would be manned by American civilian volunteers. However, for anyone with knowledge of the growing collection of American electronic equipment and, specifically, the kind of equipment put on display at the Mystic Mission demonstration, such detail is not all that important as the Sinai line will undoubtedly contain much the same package of devices modified slightly for the heat and sand of the desert environment.

Ideally, this equipment will be able to forestall hostility by the threat of detecting troop movements or weapons activities before they become dangerous, which is precisely what Henry Kissinger had in mind when he framed the plan. At its worst it could trigger false alarms thereby heightening tension—after all, much of the equipment will be on the line in a real world situation, as opposed to a test or exercise, for the first time and technical problems and misinterpretations are to be expected—or put those unarmed American technicians in a hostage situation should war break out. Nor is one hard pressed to come up with scenarios in which the sensors are tricked for some ulterior motive, say, in a case where one side wanted to give the impression that the other was acting in bad faith.

While some individual members of Congress have expressed fears about the system, there had not been any truly determined effort by Congress as of this writing to get detailed assurances from the administration that these fears were unfounded. It understates the case to say that some important questions need to be answered *in public.*

It should also be mentioned that there is more to the story of the Sinai pact than just providing electronic battlefield equipment to keep the peace. In September 1975 *The Washington Post* first revealed that in return for its signature on the agreement, Israel will be getting a number of the newest American weapons, which specifically include RPVs, laser-guided artillery shells, and other laser weapons and airborne sensing equipment.*

Another point that should be mentioned is that there is a certain Utopian promise implied by an ultimate electronic battlefield that both sides might have it out with one another without consuming any human flesh in the process. If one assumes that nations must sometimes work out their differences with hostile action, then the image of RPVs blasting each other out of the skies would be a rather pleasing and sophisticated way of contending with base, national urges. It could all become great sport and satisfy William James' unfilled order for "a moral equivalent to war." It would also conform with an idea outlined by H.G. Wells in a book called *Little Wars*. It is an elaborate war game that would be played in less than 24 hours. His contention was that "tin murder" could serve as a remedy for man's need for war. He wrote, "Let us put this prancing monarch and that silly scaremonger, all these excitable 'patriots,' and those adventurers and all the practitioners of *Weltpolitik* into one vast Temple of War, with cork carpets everywhere, and plenty of trees and little houses to knock down, and cities and fortresses, and unlimited soldiers— tons, cellarsful—and let them lead their own lives away from the rest of us."

The problem, of course, is that one cannot imagine that really happening because it would require all nations to have their own equally sophisticated electronic battlefields and agree to do all their fighting away from population centers.

---

* This would be in addition to the very sophisticated and sizable array of electronic battlefield equipment already in the hands of the Israelis. An estimate published in *Newsweek*, July 28, 1975, is that some $30 million has been spent by Israel on remote sensing equipment *alone* since the October 1973 war. The major purchase has been an electronic DEW line in the Sinai that includes such equipment as heat sensors able to note the blast of a jet taking off deep inside Egypt and display equipment that actually paints friendly blips as green circles and potentially hostile ones in red. It is no secret that when the Israelis leave the Sinai as part of the agreement, this equipment will be moved to another position. The Israelis have made it very clear that they are not going to rely entirely on American technicians to warn them of Arab transgressions.

Utopias notwithstanding, let us move to the first question, which is: will the electronic battlefield work well enough to insure that there will be no accidental, automated attacks on Americans or allied troops, no electronic My Lais, or any other misfortune brought on by technical or human error? Little has been offered by the military on the subject but actual events suggest such error is a factor. Here are three examples: (1) Well after the United States had its smart bombs in operation, American bombs fell on the French mission to Hanoi. That occurred on October 11, 1972, just after a breakthrough had been made in efforts to end the war, which is to say that it could not have happened at a worse time. No official explanation was made, but the odds seem to favor the interpretation that some electronic system was not working. (2) In 1974, Congressman Les Aspin charged that in 1971, on two separate occasions, automated transmitting systems on board submarines sent out the signal indicating that they had been "sunk by enemy action" thereby setting off a general military alert. The subs were forced to hastily surface and report by means of normal communications that it was all a false alarm. (3) Again in 1971, electronic equipment at the North American Air Defense Command (NORAD) seized control of the nationwide AP and UPI news wires indicating that an attack on the nation might be underway. "Human error"—the wrong tape was fed to a machine —caused this incident.

The question of fallibility, in turn, brings up the question of accountability. If a malfunction or human error occurs, who is responsible? Will there be a new wartime event, the technological atrocity, for which a hapless, overworked programmer some-where along the line is responsible? Will it simply be a case of going back to the drawing boards when one of the new sensors that does its own killing wipes out a village or sinks a cruise ship? This is the type of question that needs to be publicly broached.

The question of who is responsible in this kind of warfare is not just one to be addressed in the future tense because it was first raised in Vietnam. At the "Winter Soldier" hearings in which vets testified against the war, one witness who participated had this to say about the feel of automated war: "The technicians who program the computer perform no act of war, the man who places the sensor does not see it operate. The man who plots the strike never sees the plane that conducts it. The pilot, navigator, and bombardier do not see the bomb hit. The damage assessor was not in the plane, and all the others who helped mount the raid never participated in it at all."

Another major question, first asked by Senator Proxmire in 1970 in regard to the use of sensors, but which must be asked of all the elements of the electronic battlefield, is can they differentiate among soldiers, civilians, women, children, and, for that matter, soldiers carrying flags of surrender? Sensor proponents, like the experts I spoke with at the MITRE Corporation, feel the discrimination issue has been blown out of proportion. First, they argue, it takes more than one bit of sensor information to prompt an attack. If, say, a seismic and/or an acoustic sensor indicate possible enemy activity, it will require notice from a magnetic sensor that the potential target is carrying a piece of metal, presumably a gun. Secondly, they insist that it is not the sensors that behave in an indiscriminate manner but those who get their information from them (sensors don't kill, people do).

Both arguments beg the question. How, one must ask, can MAGID the merciful distinguish between a man with a gun and another with a shovel or a child fetching water in a metal pail? The second point is losing whatever little shoring it once had with the advent of Captor, SIAM, and other systems where the sensors, not other humans, order the kill.

I wrote to Senator Proxmire and asked him for his latest thinking on the issue and he replied that the matter of discrimination is "decidedly not solved at the present time." He explained, "Heat seeking devices, laser-guided weapons, and other electronic inventions as yet do not have the ability to discriminate between friend and foe except under very specific circumstances. Laser illumination of targets may help resolve this problem for the future, but at the present time, there is still great concern that weapons with independent guidance may cause havoc in a confused battlefield environment." Commenting on the specific environment of Central Europe to which much of the development of electronic battlefield devices is geared, he added, "There is bound to be a great deal of confusion on the European battlefield with troops moving here and there and civilians fleeing from the action. Thus, the issue of discrimination is heightened in this type of environment."

Is there any answer to the question of discrimination? It is of course possible to make a sensor system more and more capable of making distinctions by tacking on more and more sensors; but this makes the package on the ground larger (to say nothing of more expensive) and the larger the system the more likely it is to be discovered. A very expensive, easy-to-find piece of hardware would be the last thing the military wants. Significantly, the most discriminating sensor known to exist, the "4-Class Seismic Classifier" can only sort out what it senses into wheeled or tracked vehicle, false alarm and human being—just human being, with no attempt to say if a combatant or noncombatant is passing.

Still another issue brought forth by the electronic battlefield is one which has been raised by a number of people who point out that for all the clean sophistication of the "beep" side of the concept, the "boom" side is likely to be appalling, as the antipersonnel weapons of Igloo White and other Southeast Asian applications demonstrated so vividly. Such weaponry is not only gruesome but may be illegal to boot.

In 1972 the International Committee of the Red Cross, the group responsible for looking into oversights concerning the Geneva Convention, was told by the Red Cross to have a look at conventional weapons to see if they broke the rules. Two conferences were held to begin compiling the information needed to come up with proposals for prohibition if they were needed, while a special panel of experts met to report to the whole committee. These experts produced a report entitled *Weapons That May Cause Unnecessary Suffering or Have Indiscriminate Effects*, which is significant in that those are the terms used to describe weapons forbidden in various treaties and under the rules of war (Article 23 of the Hague Convention, for example), to which the United States has agreed. While the Red Cross report does not identify any country by name, it describes to perfection the weapons of the electronic battlefield as clearly fitting the description in the title of the report. The weapons cited included antipersonnel cluster bombs, incendiaries, antipersonnel aerial mines, and flechettes. Besides the weapons themselves, the panel also pointed to some of the delivery methods that it contended would harm more noncombatants. Time and again the expert panel—dominated by doctors and military men—did not mince words in their description of the "suffering" imposed by these weapons. This is their summary paragraph on napalm and other incendiaries:

> The injuries caused by incendiary weapons are much the same as any other burn wound, which is to say that they are exceptionally frightening and painful, difficult to treat, and likely to result in permanent deformities and disabilities. In addition, some incendiary agents superimpose their own characteristic effects upon the burn injuries. The asphyxiating and toxic properties of burning napalm and other such agents are examples of this.

As is the maddening norm in the go-slow world of international weapons control, not too much has happened since 1973 when the report was published. There was a 1974 meeting to further discuss the matter. The United States, which had refused to take part in the first two meetings, attended, but it mainly consisted of delegates giving their government's position. It will probably be several years before Sweden and the half-dozen or so other nations plumping for banning or restricting the use of such weapons actually are able to get their proposals onto the table for a vote. Whether or not a new ban—or even a reaffirmation of the rules that are being broken—will be accepted is another story. Eric Prokosch, a member of National Action Research on the Military Industrial Complex (NARMIC), a branch of the American Friends Service Committee based in Philadelphia, who attended the 1974 meeting as an official observer for the Friends World Committee for Consultation, says, "At this point the chances don't look good. It was quite obvious at the meeting that both the western and socialist nations are quite cool to the idea of giving up such weapons." *

Regardless of what comes to pass on the diplomatic front in Geneva, the point has been made by the experts' report that the United States—which is not alone, but dominates in these weapons—has been breaking rules to which it has agreed and is apparently going to continue breaking them. Using weapons against civilians is, of course, a violation of the rules, and as the experts indicated, a number of weapons have such range and dispersing ability that while they may indeed be intended to kill only those in uniform, they can hardly miss hitting civilians as well. In writing on this subject, Congressman Les Aspin has pointed out, "The power of large antipersonnel bombs—some of which blast metal particles over an area of 250 acres—makes it inevitable that civilians will be injured or killed." Nor does it require a panel of experts to see that some weapons cause unnecessary suffering. Dr. Philip Harvey, a British doctor in Hanoi during American raids on April 16, 1972, has reported the

---

* Prokosch, by the way, was fascinated by the extreme cordiality of this meeting where the most grisly of weapons were discussed. In deference to the United States, he reports, the war in Vietnam was never referred to by name but rather as "a recent conflict." Obviously, nobody at the Geneva meeting had stepped on a Dragontooth mine.

discovery of a new way of adding suffering to suffering. He found that plastic pellets had been used to replace metal ones in antipersonnel weapons. The advantages of these are that they cannot be located by normal X-ray and that they move at speeds of 1,300 feet per second creating such intense heat that they vaporize human flesh. "They can fracture bone without even making contact with it," he reported after examining some of the plasticized victims.

The suggestion has been made that the increased accuracy and control of laser-guided and other smart ordnance will mitigate the problem somewhat because of greater accuracy. However, a number of people, Aspin and Harvey Brooks of Harvard among them, point out that historically, greater accuracy has always brought with it an increased rate of delivery—doubling every eight to ten years by the Pentagon's own accounting. Aspin sums up the argument: "Despite the ever-improving accuracy of our weapons, the 'collateral' damage—that is, the damage to civilians and their property—has constantly increased."

Then there is the issue that really transcends and to varying degrees encompasses the others, which is that this major development is taking place without question or examination from the public or its representatives. Congress has expressed only intermittent interest and much of that has been adulatory, such as Senator Goldwater's comparison of it to the discovery of gunpowder. An even more telling development came in the spring of 1974 when the Senate Armed Services Committee decided to examine the new electronic gadgets and held an extra round of hearings on them. All the chirps and blips so impressed the Committee that it actually chided the Department of Defense research boss Malcolm R. Currie for not having requested "enough" money for supporting the technology base from which such marvels spring. Just about the only critic who has really tackled the issue and asked hard questions is Proxmire, but his comments on the matter have been negligible since 1970 and 1971 when his interest was keenest. As has just been shown, the issues raised by Proxmire then are still valid and in need of much deeper scrutiny.

Before American troops left Vietnam the electronic battlefield was attracting the attention of antiwar and peace research groups, but almost all of that interest died away when the US withdrew. The only major, sustained effort to educate the public about the electronic battlefield has been by NARMIC. Its major effort at public education in this matter began in 1972 with the production and distribution of some 1,300 copies of a filmstrip and script entitled "The Automated Air War," which concentrated mainly on Igloo White. It was widely shown in the United States, Canada, and Europe. The NARMIC exposé is a well-documented, strong condemnation of the electronic battlefield innovations used in Southeast Asia.

NARMIC has also issued periodic reports and press releases that were clearly intended to make news for the electronic battlefield and heighten the public's sensibilities. For instance, in response to Richard Nixon's 1971 troop withdrawals and his "winding down" of the war, it issued a 19 page background report attempting to show that as the men were withdrawn, machines were replacing them, and that a full-scale war was now being carried out by remote control.

For a time, and in large part due to NARMIC, the electronic battlefield became a focal point for those opposed to the war. "A moral outrage," said Senator George McGovern. "As our ground forces are withdrawn, Indochina for us is becoming as much a laboratory as a battlefield, with Asians serving as guinea pigs in our tests of deadly new technology." Lists of electronic battlefield contractors, complete with the brand names of consumer products they make, were distributed by peace groups who urged others to boycott those products. In Boston, the Non-Violent Direct Action Group held a "Magical Mystery Tour" of "informational picket lines" in front of area weapons contractors' plants and research facilities to draw attention to the automated battlefield. In Hawaii, three men broke into the offices of the Pacific Air Force at Hickam Air Force Base and poured their own blood into files containing classified information on the use of electronics in Southeast Asia. Much hostile attention was focused on the Jasons who had started the whole thing. These scientists were singled out for attack by antiwar groups and editorialists who saw them as the embodiment of all that was inhumane and immoral about a lousy war in which people who had never seen an American face were dying from bombs dropped from planes by computer. One group of technically oriented dissidents, Scientists and Engineers for Social and Political Action, took on the Jasons in one broadside after another, calling them, among many other things, "a significant force directed against the interest of world peace." Peter Stubbs, editor of *New Scientist*, in an editorial pointed most directly at the physicist-dominated Jasons, said, "It was physicists who produced laser bombing; it was physicists who invented the electronic battlefield; it was physicists who devised plastic antipersonnel bombs, 'gravel', 'spider mines', 'daisy cutters'—and a plethora of other perversions. Why shouldn't the public distrust them as a race? They do little to purge their ranks of the monsters who contrive such appalling inhumanities." More than mere words were needed by others to express their indignation: the Physics Building at Columbia University was occupied in protest of Jasons from that campus; a Jason outraged a group of French scientists for his contribution to the war; and large protests were held when five Jasons appeared for an international symposium on physics in Trieste.* To many who actively opposed the war

---

* Certain Jasons must have found all of this quite disconcerting because of their own positions on the war. British physicist B.H.S. Burhop surveyed the Jasons on their feelings towards the war in general and the electronic line in particular and discovered that several of them claimed to have abhorred the war and only worked on the barrier to "enable the (ineffective) bombing to stop and would thus save lives and also make possible an early US withdrawal." Burhop adds, "This argument did not appeal to all the Jason participants,

the name Jason still carries the most diabolical connotation.

Of all the criticism, however, some of the harshest and sharpest came from those who had participated in Igloo White and other portions of the electronic war. The "Winter Soldier" hearings staged in 1972 by the Vietnam Veterans Against the War on the conduct of the war mainly concentrated on the testimony of "grunts"—men on the ground who had actually been face to face with the enemy—but one part of the proceedings was reserved for the pilots, programmers, ordnance technicians, and others who wished to report on the electronic battlefield and auto-mated air war. The gist of all this testimony was presented in an opening statement by Vietnam veteran Eric Herter, grandson of the former Secretary of State Christian Herter, which said in part:

We have been participants in the new forms of war that are to replace the unpopular struggle of infantry and patrol against guerrilla bands. Replace it with a greater atrocity than a hundred My Lais: the systematic destruction of thousands of innocent persons, of entire cultures by an automated electronic and mechanical death machine whose killing will be one-sided, unseen and universal. Those of us who testify are aware of the degree to which this hellish future is already upon us. We have seen the mechanical monster, the mindless devastation, the agony of simple people caught in the fire storm of our technological rampage.

Strong words, but Herter was deeply and genuinely disturbed by a new form of war and what it could do to people pushing "kill" buttons, eliminating even the "tortured bond of humanity between enemies at war." He explained how it was to work with the electronic battlefield in its first war: "Under its auspices, the

---

however. One wrote that he did not work on the electronic fence because 'the idea of attempting to solve essentially political problems by military means or electronic gimmickry repelled me.' "

people of the villages have gone from being 'gooks' and 'dinks' to being grid-coordinates, blips on scan screens, dots of light on infrared film. They are never seen, never known, never even hated. The machine functions, the radar blip disappears. No village is destroyed, no humans die. For none existed.''

Despite such protestations and the work of NARMIC, most Americans have very little if any knowledge of the system. Even many of those who are aware of the electronic battlefield or know of what went on in Southeast Asia, still do not understand its size and importance to the military today or its cost to the nation in the post-Vietnam era—something about which the Pentagon is not issuing press releases. The general public aside, there are undoubtedly some engineers and scientists working on parts of today's electronic dream who are not aware of how their work fits into the larger military scheme. And as for Congress, one has to go back to 1970 when Proxmire said, "Most members of the Senate I have talked to did not even know that we had such a program," for the key to this situation. While that has changed mainly because of the hearings held later that year, it would appear from reading more recent hearings on military matters and the *Congressional Record* that Congress has not bothered to have a critical— or even mildly investigative—look at how the system has fared since then. Those aforementioned special Senate Armed Services hearings on electronic innovation held in 1974 (after which the Committee told the Pentagon it had not asked for enough money) were more in the nature of a testimonial banquet in honor of the new technology at which were heard very few discouraging words.

There are some rather specific reasons that suggest themselves for this lack of concern and interest. An important one is that the electronic battlefield is a loose concept rather than a cohesive program with its own central office, research directorate, and so forth. Thus, it does not appear as a line item in military budget requests, and since there is no budget or timetable for it there can be no cost overruns or delays to attract attention. Indeed, members of Congress have questioned the cost, concept and need for such specific items as magnetic sensors in the Army budget, AWACS, and others, but it appears that the gigantic parent concept has been too elusive to question as a whole. There is also a large Catch-22 possibility lurking in all of this. For several years now the military has seldom used the terms electronic or automated battlefield in its official presentations and budget documents—although both terms are in common use in informal conversations. Should some heat be focused on the electronic battlefield, the military would only have to say that there is no such thing.

A more important reason for the unquestioned growth of the electronic battlefield, however, may stem from the very neat way it fits into the concept of a smaller, volunteer armed force with fewer and fewer men stationed overseas, which has been strongly supported by the White House (both Nixon and Ford) and most members of Congress over the last few years. As the electronic battlefield is further adapted for application in Europe there is little question that some of those troops in Germany who irk so many politicians will be able to come home, replaced in the field by RPVs, sensors, and computers.

Perhaps the most important factor, though, is the way the electronic battlefield will fit into future wars in terms of domestic American politics and realities. By creating a way of war that depends on fewer and fewer American boys it is easier, in terms of public acceptance, for the nation to become involved in conflicts around the globe. Much of the anger felt at home over United States involvement in Vietnam was centered on American casualties. There would be far less anger directed against an encounter in which the United States was putting hardware, not men, on the line and in which American casualty lists were dominated by decimated sensors, burnt-out computers, and downed RPVs. In personnel terms, a sensor is a soldier able to do the most exacting reconnaissance work; it does not sleep, know fear, bleed, eat, or disobey. Similarly, a logistics computer replaces several officers and a bevy of clerks, a Grasshopper bomb has the effect of a unit of boobytrappers, Captor is a submarine on station that needs no men to sit around breathing precious air . . . and so forth through the various elements of the whole. Besides cutting down on the number of men required to run a war, the electronic battlefield also promises to shorten radically the time used from the start to the finish of a military action. That the disillusionment with and the protest over the longest war in American history grew as a function of time was not missed by the military, which is now determined to have such precise, time-saving things as ordnance that never, or at least rarely, misses.

It would seem that the major point underscored by the continuing development of the electronic battlefield is: the lesson of Vietnam is not that it was a moral, tactical, and economic outrage, but that it was *inefficient.* The electronic battlefield that took shape during the waning days of that war is now embellished and refined to make war more efficient for the next generation.

Because the concept of the electronic battlefield has not been seriously questioned by civilian America, either through its Congress or by other means, it has become a national goal of the highest order and priority set by the military, its research associates, and contractors—that is, with a permissive wink from Congress.

There is a final logical question. Is not this new kind of war just a bit too easy to wage? That is, is the electronic battlefield so compact, fast, and mobile that war becomes a minor surgical procedure that does not disturb the body politic to any great extent? The spectre of Vietnam again has relevance because it is safe to assume that the last thing the nation's leaders want is another prolonged nightmare involving more than a half-million men. Actions more in the style and speed of the *Mayaguez* incident (albeit with fewer men and casualties) would seem to be the kind of thing best suited to the electronic battlefield. Protecting American lives in war is a goal without question; but one must actively question a system that is so efficient that it makes war a more attractive option because it limits losses to a very few or no American deaths. The temptation for a nation with the capacity to wage what amounts to a painless (for the home team at least) porta-war could be great.

Increasingly, however, this and the other questions raised here will become questions of academic interest only because the electronic battlefield will become a greater and greater reality. The plans are drawn, the multibillion-dollar down payment has been made, parts of it have already been tested in a real war, and the rest of the wiring is going in right now.

CHRONOLOGY OF IMPORTANT
ELECTRONIC BATTLEFIELD EVENTS

September 13, 1960—The First Air Force Bionics Symposium.

September 15, 1966—Defense Communications Planning Group created to develop the "McNamara Line."

July 16, 1967—Beaches near Eglin Air Force Base, Florida, evacuated because of button bomblets washing into the area from test site.

December, 1967—Igloo White becomes operational in Southeast Asia.

January 18, 1968—Sensors offered to Marines holding Khe Sanh. They are emplanted and in operation within 48 hours.

January 21, 1968—Attack on Khe Sanh begins.

January 31, 1968—Tet Offensive begins.

March 19, 1969—New Defense Secretary Melvin Laird announces cancellation of the original McNamara Line. This creates the impression that the whole effort has been in vain.

October 14, 1969—General William C. Westmoreland delivers his key "Electronic Battlefield" speech to the annual meeting of the Association of the United States Army in Washington, D.C.

June 5–8, 1969—Battle at Fire Base Crook.

January 7, 1970—Secret industry briefing on "warfare of the future" given at the National Bureau of Standards.

January 31, 1970—*Business Week* states that the electronic battlefield has already cost $2 billion and may cost a total of $20 billion by the year 1980.

July 6, 1970—Senator William Proxmire first raises financial, moral and tactical questions about the electronic battlefield.

July 13–August 17, 1970—Colloquy between Proxmire and Senator Barry Goldwater on the electronic battlefield during which Goldwater terms it "probably the greatest step forward in warfare since gunpowder."

August 20, 1970—Senate Armed Services Committee and General

Accounting Office studies of the electronic battlefield both ordered on this day.

November 18, 19, and 24, 1970—Senate Electronic Battlefield Subcommittee Hearings held.

December 12, 1970—Deputy Defense Secretary David Packard orders DCPG to develop sensors and associated equipment for European use.

January 1, 1971—DCPG turns over Igloo White to the Air Force.

Early 1971—A Ryan remotely piloted vehicle (RPV) scores a direct "hit" on a manned F-4 Phantom in a simulated "dogfight" over the Pacific Test Range.

March 1, 1971—Final report of the special Senate Electronic Battlefield Subcommittee.

Spring, 1971—Laser-guided or "smart" bombs first used in combat in Vietnam on a limited basis.

March, 1972—First large-scale use of laser-guided bombs in combat.

May 15–29, 1972—Mystic Mission display of electronic battlefield held in Germany.

June 30, 1972—DCPG (now DSPG for Defense Special Projects Group) closes.

March, 1974—Defense Research Chief Malcolm Currie announces "a true revolution in conventional warfare."

May, 1975—U-2 crashes in Germany revealing a new departure in automated battlefield technology.

APPENDIX A

Address by
General W. C. Westmoreland
Chief Of Staff, United States Army
Annual Luncheon
Association Of The United States Army
Sheraton Park Hotel, Washington, D. C.
Tuesday, October 14, 1969

I always welcome the opportunity to address those who support this Association . . . I know I am among friends who are vitally concerned about our Army.

Our Army today is a dynamic organization undergoing change to stay abreast of a rapidly changing technology and society.

In our adult lifetime many of us have witnessed change unequalled in history—the jet airplane, nuclear power, television, and the computer—to name a few. And the social change that *should have* come within the last century has been our legacy to accomplish in our generation—*now*.

As an integral part of our changing society, the Army has also been challenged to meet those demands. We in the Army accept the challenge . . . just as we have accepted and met all our challenges in the past.

Today our Army is weathering a period not too unlike others in our proud history.

Today once again the fundamental principles of our profession—the pillars of discipline on which an Army is built—the trust and confidence that have traditionally motivated the soldier are being questioned. We cannot this time wait for a call to action. The problems that we must address exist within our own ranks . . . we share them with the entire Nation. With our troubled society questioning the role of the Army more

215

than ever before, each soldier in a position of leadership is on trial . . . both his character and his integrity are being tested. To meet the test, he must stand on his principles . . . his personal and professional code of ethics, his dedication, his leadership. These are the principles that resolve the crucial . . . these determine the worth of a man's life. These are the hallmarks of the professional soldier in his finest tradition.

The U. S. Army has served its country proudly. It continues to respond to legally constituted executive authority. But the American people also must understand that their Army does not exist to fight without something to fight for. Our Armed Forces on the international scene are as necessary for the security of our country as our domestic police forces are necessary for law and order at home. Our Army can only be as effective as the spirit of its soldiers. And certainly this spirit is sparked by public trust, support, and confidence.

The Army is as dedicated now as it has been for nearly two centuries . . . dedicated to the preservation of our way of life. In guarding this trust, we have never failed. What more could a country ask of its soldiers?

Recently, a few individuals involved in serious incidents have been highlighted in the news. Some would have these incidents reflect on the Army as a whole. They are, however, the actions of a pitiful few. Certainly the Army cannot and will not condone improper conduct or criminal acts—and I personally assure you that I will not. We will always regard the rights of the individual and acknowledge due process of law. But the Army as an institution should never be put on trial as we deal with the few.

We are a proud Army. We do have confidence in our officers, noncommissioned officers, and soldiers who continue to provide the Army and the Nation with the selfless devoted service that has always been our cherished tradition.

This year, I take special satisfaction in addressing this audience—for I know you are dedicated to the maintenance of a strong, modern Army through military-industrial-labor-academic-scientific cooperation. This team provides the Armed Forces with the best equipment science and technology can produce. This cooperative effort is an element of national power that must never be eroded.

For this reason, I will focus now on purely military matters . . . on developments that are of special interest to this audience.

I will proceed on the assumption that neither the Congress nor the Nation wants us to lay down our shield of armed readiness. On the contrary, our citizens continue to demand from us the best military forces possible within the resources made available to us. This is a fair and demanding challenge which we accept.

In meeting this challenge, the Army has undergone in Vietnam a quiet revolution in ground warfare—tactics, techniques, and technology. This revolution is not fully understood by many. To date it has received only limited attention. Analysis of the lessons from this revolution will influence the future direction of our Army both in fundamental concepts of organization and development of equipment.

When the first American units were committed in Vietnam, they were to a large extent a reflection of the organization, tactics, techniques, and technology of World War II, with one noteworthy exception. That exception, of course, was best demonstrated by the 1st Air Cavalry Division. For the first time, an Army unit of division size had been organized and equipped to free itself from the constrictions of terrain through the use of battlefield air mobility. The concept and resultant organization were logical outgrowths of the development of sturdy, reliable helicopters for troops carriers, weapons platforms, command and control, aerial ambulances, and reconnaissance vehicles and larger helicopters for carrying artillery, ammunition, and supplies. Even before the arrival of American combat troops, the effective use of the helicopter had been demonstrated in the support of the Vietnamese. I am confident that the vitality of air mobility is recognized and understood by this informed audience.

We learned that Vietnam posed a problem even more difficult than mobility. The enemy we face in Vietnam is naturally elusive and cunning in his use of the dense jungle for concealment. As a result, in the early days of the American commitment we found ourselves with an abundance of firepower and mobility. But we were limited in our ability to locate the enemy. We were not quite a giant without eyes, but that allusion had some validity. Whenever we engaged the enemy, we won the battle. Too often those battles were at enemy initiative and not our own.

Too often battles were not fought because the enemy could not be found or because, after initial contact, he had slipped elusively into the jungle or across borders politically beyond our reach . . . or had literally gone underground.

Since 1965 a principal thrust of our experimentation, adaptation and development in tactics, techniques, and technology has been toward improvement of our capability to find the enemy. Each year of the war witnessed substantial improvement. In 1965, 1966, 1967, and early 1968 we increased the number of both air and ground cavalry units. We added a second airmobile division. As our troops arrived, we progressively organized special reconnaissance elements of all kinds, including long-range patrol companies and special forces teams. We found ourselves more and more using the infantry for the purpose of finding the enemy. When the enemy broke down into small units, we did likewise. We learned to operate skillfully at night. We mastered the enemy's ambush techniques. Technical means were reinforced and improved. Intelligence organizations were expanded and refined.

During this period, the Director of Defense Research and Engineering urged the scientific community to develop a new family of sensors and associated communications equipment to help locate enemy forces on infiltration routes. After proving these devices workable in test, we developed plans in 1967 to use them throughout the battlefield. In mid 1968, our field experiments began. Since then, we have integrated these new devices with the more conventional surveillance equipment and other intelligence collection means. As a result, our ability to find the enemy has improved materially.

Comparing the past few years of progress with a forecast of the future produces one conclusion: we are on the threshold of an entirely new battlefield concept.

Now let me briefly examine the past and relate it to the future.

The Napoleonic Wars are well documented in history texts. Firepower was limited. Mobility was limited essentially to the foot soldier. Support services were provided by contract or foraging. Cavalry, scouts and pickets provided intelligence. This chapter of military history is replete with numerous examples of battles that might have been . . . had the opposing forces known of each other's presence. But when forces made contact, they massed to do battle. At Waterloo, for example, over 140,000 troops crowded into less than three miles of front line contact.

A little over a century later, World War I brought trench warfare. The advent of the machine gun and massed artillery introduced sizeable increases in the firepower capabilities available to ground forces. Mobility and support efforts experienced little change. Maneuver on the battlefield was almost nonexistent. Only a few visionaries saw any real utility in the tank. Primitive aerial observation brought only marginal improvements in intelligence gathering. The density of troops in the front line, reduced from that of Waterloo, still remained high as soldiers crowded shoulder to shoulder in their network of trenches. Without mobility and information about the enemy, the newly acquired firepower served little purpose.

World War II saw the tank mature, and armies organized to capitalize on this capability. Mobility began to gain on firepower. While the Navy was developing sonar and air elements proceeded with intercept radars, Army target acquisition systems remained essentially at the World War I level. The wheeled vehicle improved our support effort. But we were still confined to the ground with our airlift capability remaining minimal.

The increased mobility, however, did permit combat elements to disperse over a wider front, and the density of troops along the battle lines became smaller. Still, the absence of a refined intelligence capability permitted only small economies of force.

But the Vietnam War has seen a revolution in ground force mobility. We no longer assign units a sector of frontage. Instead, units are responsible for an operational area. And with the mobility of the helicopter, units like the 1st Cavalry and the 101st Airborne Divisions cover hundreds of square miles with their airmobile blankets.

The revolution I envision for the future comes not from the helicopter alone, but from systems that heretofore have been unknown.

For a moment, let us consider the basic combat role of the Army. As the Nation's land force, our mission is to defeat enemy forces in land combat and to gain control of the land and its people. In this role, we have traditionally recognized five functions. But we have emphasized only three: mobility, firepower, and command and control—in other words—move, shoot, and communicate. To me, the other two—intelligence and support—have not been sufficiently stressed. Placing the functions in proper perspective, I visualize the Army's job in land combat as:

+ First, we must find the enemy.
+ Second, we must destroy the enemy.
+ And third, we must support the forces that perform the other two functions.

By studying operations in Vietnam, one can better understand these functions.

Large parts of the infantry, ground and air cavalry, and aviation are used in what I will now call "STANO"—surveillance, target acquisition and night observation, or function number one—finding the enemy. In this function large areas can be covered continuously by aerial surveillance systems, unattended ground sensors, radars and other perfected means of finding the enemy. These systems can permit us to deploy our fires and forces more effectively in the most likely and most productive areas.

The second function—destroying the enemy—is the role of our combat forces—artillery, air, armor, and infantry, together with the helicopters needed to move the combat troops. Firepower can be concentrated without massing large numbers of troops. In Vietnam where artillery and tactical air forces inflict over two-thirds of the enemy casualties, firepower is responsive as never before. It can rain destruction anywhere on the battlefield within minutes . . . whether friendly troops are present or not.

Inherent in the function of destroying the enemy is fixing the enemy. In the past, we have devoted sizeable portions of our forces to this requirement. In the future, however, fixing the enemy will become a problem primarily in time rather than space. More specifically, if one knows continually the location of his enemy and has the capability to mass fires instantly, he need not necessarily fix the enemy in one location with forces on the ground. On the battlefield of the future, enemy forces will be located, tracked, and targeted almost instantaneously through the use of data links, computer assisted intelligence evaluation, and automated fire control. With first round kill probabilities approaching certainty, and with surveillance devices that can continually track the enemy, the need for large forces to fix the opposition physically will be less important.

Although the future portends a more automated battlefield, we do visualize a continuing need for highly mobile forces to surround, canalize, block or otherwise maneuver an enemy into the most lucrative target.

The third function includes an improved communicative system. This system not only would permit commanders to be continually aware of the entire battlefield panorama down to squad and platoon level, but would permit logistics systems to rely more heavily on air lines of communications.

Today, machines and technology are permitting economy of manpower on the battlefield, as indeed they are in the factory. But the future offers even more possibilities for economy. I am confident the American people expect this country to take full advantage of its technology—to welcome and applaud the developments that will replace wherever possible the man with the machine.

Based on our total battlefield experience and our proven technological capability, I foresee a new battlefield array.

+ I see battlefields or combat areas that are under 24 hour real or near real time surveillance of all types.
+ I see battlefields on which we can destroy anything we locate through instant communications and the almost instantaneous application of highly lethal firepower.
+ I see a continuing need for highly mobile combat forces to assist in fixing and destroying the enemy.

The changed battlefield will dictate that the supporting logistics system also undergo change.

+ I see the forward end of the logistics system with mobility equal to the supported force.

+ I see the elimination of many intermediate support echelons and the use of inventory-in-motion techniques.
+ I see some Army forces supported by air—in some instances directly from bases here in the continental United States.

In both the combat and support forces of the future, I see a continuing need for our traditionally highly skilled, well-motivated individual soldier . . . the soldier who has always responded in time of crisis—and the soldier who will accept and meet the challenges of the future.

Currently, we have hundreds of surveillance, target acquisition, night observation and information processing systems either in being, in development or in engineering. These range from field computers to advanced airborne sensors and new night vision devices.

Our problem now is to further our knowledge—exploit our technology, and equally important—to incorporate all these devices into an integrated land combat system.

History has reinforced my conviction that major advances in the art of warfare have grown from the Fullers and Guderians—men who detected, in the slow, clumsy, underarmed, largely ineffective tanks of World War I, the seeds of the future. Between the two World Wars, they foresaw with clarity the blitzkrieg of armored and panzer forces that introduced a new dimension to ground warfare.

More recently, Generals Howze and Wheeler and the late Lieutenant General Bill Bunker conceived air mobility long before the machinery existed to fulfill the concept. Today we witness both the airmobile concept and the airmobile division proved in Vietnam.

We are confident that from our early solutions to the problem of finding the enemy, in Vietnam the evidence is present to visualize this battlefield of the future . . . a battlefield that will dictate organizations and techniques radically different from those we have now.

In summary, I see an Army built into and around an integrated area control system that exploits the advanced technology of communications, sensors, fire direction, and the required automatic data processing —a system that is sensitive to the dynamics of the ever-changing battlefield—a system that materially assists the tactical commander in making sound and timely decisions.

To achieve this concept of our future Army, we have established, at the Department of Army Staff level, a Systems Manager, Brigadier General Bill Fulton, to coordinate all Army activities in this field. We have done this because of problem complexity. We are dealing with systems that are fundamental to the Army—its doctrine, its organization, and its equipment. We are on the threshold for the first time in achieving maximum utilization of both our firepower and our mobility. In order to succeed in this effort, we need the scientific and engineering support of both the military and the industrial communities.

To complement the systems management, we are establishing at Fort Hood a test facility through which new equipment, new organizations, and new techniques can be subjected to experimentation, adaptation, evaluation, and integration. This facility will be headed by Major General Jack Norton who will report to the Project Director, Lieutenant General Bev Powell, III Corps Commander and Commanding General, Fort Hood.

Hundreds of years were required to achieve the mobility of the armored division. A little over two decades later we had the airmobile division. With cooperative effort, no more than 10 years should separate us from the automated battlefield.

Some will say that this is an unrealistic expectation. Some will say that the current experience in Vietnam, in which the infantry continues to bear the brunt of combat, does not support this visualization of the future. History tells another story. The experience and technology at the time of the British Mark IV tank at Cambrai in 1917 and the H-34 helicopter in the fifties provided the evidence to define the future of these systems.

I believe our future path has been clearly blazed.

We will pioneer this new dimension in ground warfare and develop an integrated battlefield system. The United States Army will again lead the way. Our young officers and NCO's will accept the challenge.

APPENDIX B

PARTIAL LISTING OF ELECTRONIC BATTLEFIELD CONTRACTORS.

Aerojet General
Aerospace
ALCOA
American Machine and Foundry (AMF)
Analytics
Avco
Barnes Engineering
Beech Aircraft
Boeing
Chrysler
Control Data
Datacom
Davidson Optronics
Dorsett Electronics
E Systems
EDO
Electrospace
ENSCO
Environmental Research Institute of Michigan
FMC
Ford Motor
Garrett
General Autronics
General Dynamics
General Electric
General Telephone and Electronics

GTE-Sylvania
General Motors
Goodyear Aerospace
Grumman Aerospace
Harris
Hazeltine
Honeywell
Hughes Aircraft
Hughes Tool
IBM
Institute for Defense Analyses
International Telephone and Telegraph
Johns Hopkins Applied Physics Laboratory
Kaiser Aerospace and Electronics
Lear Siegler
Litton Guidance and Control Systems
Litton Industries
Lockheed Aircraft
LTV Aerospace
Magnavox
Melpar
Minnesota Mining and Manufacturing
MITRE
Motorola
McDonnell Douglas Astronautics
McDonnell Douglas

North American Philips
Northrop
Philco-Ford
Power Conversion
RAND
Raytheon
RCA
Research Analysis
Rockwell International
Sandia
Scope
Scoville Manufacturing
Singer Aerospace and Marine Systems
Sperry Rand
Stanford Research Institute

System Development
Teledyne-Ryan Aeronautical
Texas Instruments
Textron
Thiokol Chemical
Tracor
T.R.-Mallory
TRW
United Aircraft
Varian Associates
Varo
Western Electric
Westinghouse Electric
Xerox
Zenith Radio

BIBLIOGRAPHY

Aerospace. "A New Breed of Super Servants: Remotely Piloted Vehicles." February, 1975.

Aerospace Daily. "Air Force Studies Improved 'Igloo White' System; Sees World-Wide Applications." January 21, 1971.

—— "Laser Weapons on Rise at Pentagon." December 6, 1974.

—— "Natural Barrier." October 21, 1968.

—— "Southeast Asian Tactical Sensor Budget Put at $200 Million." August 4, 1970.

—— "U-2 Mission: Radar Location 'Automated Battlefield' Techniques." June 2, 1975.

Air Force. "Air Force Almanac." May, 1974.

—— Special sections on "The Electronic Air Force" appearing in the July, 1971, and July, 1974 issues.

Air Force Association. "Policy Resolutions for 1974–75." Adopted at the National Convention in Washington, D.C., on September 16, 1974.

Allman, T.D. "The Blind Bombers." *Far Eastern Economic Review*, January 29, 1972.

Alsop, Joseph. "Outcome of B-52s New Battle Will Determine Abrams' Plan." *Washington Post*, February 19, 1969.

Andelman, David A. "US Implanting an Electronic 'Fence' to Shut Mexican Border to Smuggling." *New York Times*, July 14, 1973.

Anderson, Jack. "Indochina Jungle Sown With Sensors." *Washington Post*, July 10, 1970.

Apple, R.W., Jr. "Johnson Reaches Guam for Parley on Vietnam War." *New York Times*, March 21, 1967.

Arbuckle, Tammy. "Ho Trail Hides Its Traffic." *The Sunday Star*, March 7, 1971.

Ardman, Harvey. "How Vietnam Tested US Army Planning." *The American Legion Magazine*, February, 1970.

—— "The Great 'Robot' Arms Race." *The American Legion Magazine*, October, 1972.

Armed Forces Journal. "AC-130 Gunships Destroy Trucks and Cargo." September, 1971.

—— "Army Unveils Project MASSTER." May 9, 1970.

—— "DoD's New DSPG to Counter SAM Defenses." April 18, 1971.

—— "Hobo Kit Makes Iron Bombs into Guided Missiles." March 1, 1971.

Armed Forces Management. "Intelligence: the Lagging Function." May, 1970.

Army Research and Development News Magazine. "MASSTER to Evaluate Canadian CL-89 Drone Aircraft as Search for High-Performance RPV System Resumes." September, 1972.

Army Times. "Mum's Word on Barrier, Mac Orders." September 20, 1967.

———— "Touch of Hollywood Comes to Huachuca." March 10, 1971.

Ashworth, George W. "Viet Barrier—Test for McNamara." *Christian Science Monitor*, November 6, 1967.

Aspin, Les. "Not So Conventional." *New York Times*, August 23, 1973.

Associated Press. "Laos is Said to Plan Electronic Line to Halt Foe." *New York Times*, January 24, 1968.

———— "Mini Mines Drift Onto Florida Beach." *Washington Evening Star*, July 17, 1967.

———— "Proxmire Scores Pentagon's Electronic Detector." *New York Times*, July 6, 1970.

———— "Saigon Troops to Run US Sensors." *Washington Sunday Star*, June 15, 1969.

Aviation Week and Space Technology. "Army Flight Tests to Explore Mini-RPV Battlefield Role." March 3, 1975.

———— "Multiple Roles Likely for Drone Aircraft." February 21, 1972.

Baldwin, Hanson W. "US Adding 12 Miles to Vietnam Barrier Strip." *New York Times*, July 21, 1967.

Barkan, Robert. "Bringing the Toys Home." *Pacific Research and World Empire Telegram*, November-December, 1971.

———— "Nobody Here But Us Robots." *The New Republic*, April 29, 1972.

———— "Science Fiction—or Tomorrow's US?" *Guardian*, October 27, 1971.

Barker, Ben C., Jr. "Joint-Service Intrusion Detection System." Paper produced by US Army Mobility Equipment Research and Development Center, Fort Belvoir, Va. 22060 n.d.

Beecher, William. "Pentagon Pushing 'Bugging' Devices." *New York Times*, March 25, 1972.

———— "Sensor 'Seal' Around Vietnam Studied." *New York Times*, February 13, 1970.

Berent, Lt. Col. Mark E. "A Group Called Wolf." *Air Force*, February, 1971.

Blumenthal, Ralph. "Electronic Sensors Foil Unseen Enemy." *New York Times*, February 18, 1970.

Boston Sunday Globe. "Senate Probing How the Military Misplaced Millions." December 5, 1971.

Boulle, Pierre. *Ears of the Jungle.* New York: Vanguard Press, 1972.

Branfman, Fred. "The Era of the Blue Machine, Laos: 1969." *Washington Monthly*, July, 1971.

Brossard, Chandler. "Why the Death Machine Could Die Laughing." *Penthouse*, April, 1972.

Brown, Gen. George S. *United States Military Posture for Fiscal Year 1976.* Washington, D.C., the Pentagon, January, 1975.

Brown, J.J. "Sensors Still Do Not Stop North Vietnamese Forces." Dispatch News Service International (DNSI), June 12, 1972.
——— "US Electronic Boondoggles in Indochina." DNSI, June 2, 1972.
Browne, Malcolm W. "Sensors Give a Thai Air Base an Ear to the Ground of Ho Chi Minh Trail." *New York Times*, October 23, 1972.
Burgess, John. "Unplugging Electronic Battlefields." *San Francisco Chronicle*, September 16, 1972.
Burhop, E.H.S. "Scientists and Soldiers." *Bulletin of the Atomic Scientists*, n.d.
Burke, Col. John T. " 'Smart' Weapons; A Coming Revolution in Tactics." *Army*, February, 1973.
Burkett, Warren. "Electronic Battlefield Draws Scrutiny on Hill." *Product Engineering*, February 16, 1970.
Business Week. "The Pentagon Plays Electronic War Games." January 31, 1970.
Canan, James W. *The Superwarriors.* New York: Weybright & Talley, 1975.
Carter, Phillip D. "Goldwater Assails 'Gnomes' of Capital." *Washington Post*, July 15, 1970.
Clark, Evert. "Top Scientist Cuts All Links to War." *New York Times*, March 1, 1968.
Clark, Mike. "Electronics Moves from War in Vietnam." *Philadelphia Inquirer*, February 20, 1972.
Clawson, Ken W. "US Testing Sensors Along Mexican Border." *Washington Post*, July 18, 1970.
Cohen, S.T. "A Flash Bulb Approach to Some Vietnam Defense Problems." Santa Monica, California. The RAND Corp., April, 1967.
Commander's Digest. "Accurate Detection, Location of Enemy a Must." "Basic Concepts of Sensor Systems." "J-SIID Sensors Detect Room Penetration." "Igloo White: A Cool Airborne Sensoring System." "Sensor Technology Used in Vietnam." "Army Develops New Sophisticated Sensors." "Marines' First Real Test of Remote Sensors." "Naval Use of Sensors in SEA Began in 1968." September 20, 1973.
——— "Deployment, Use of Electronic Sensors are Explained." February 27, 1971.
——— "Fighting With Bullets Instead of Bodies." January 16, 1971.
——— "Worldwide Military Command and Control." Special issue, February 14, 1974.
Congressional Record. Pages Covering Senate Electronic Battlefield Discussion. July 6, 1970 (S.10545–6), July 13, 1970 (S.11102–15), July 14, 1970 (S.24107–08), July 31, 1970 (S.26766–72), August 17, 1970 (S.29181–3), November 23, 1970 (S.18711–15), March 23, 1971 (S.3618–22).
Connolly, Ray. "Intrusion Detectors Score in Laos." *Electronics*, March 15, 1971.
——— "Pilotless Planes: Big New Market?" *Electronics*, July 31, 1972.
Craig, G. and Hirsch, S. *Mystic Mission: Sensor System Briefings.* Washington, D.C., the MITRE Corp., June 30, 1972.

Craig, G. and Svedlow, J. *Mystic Mission: Exhibits.* Washington, D.C., the
MITRE Corp., June 30, 1972.
David, Heather M. "Army Drawing Remote Sensor Specs." *Electronic News,*
May 4, 1970.
Davis, MSGT. Raymond. "REMBASS . . . New Dimension in Battlefield
Intelligence." *Arrowhead,* February, 1972.
Davis, Richard T. "Smart Bombs Perform Interdiction Surgery." *Microwaves,*
October, 1972.
Deane, Maj. Gen. John R., Jr. Transcript of Press Briefing on Igloo White.
Washington, D.C., the Pentagon, February 17, 1971.
de Borchgrave, Arnaud. "How to End the Bombing and De-Escalate." *News-
week,* May 15, 1967.
Deepe, Beverly. "Tactical Nose—People Sniffer Peers Beneath Vietnam Foli-
age." *Christian Science Monitor,* September 26, 1968.
Dickson, Paul and Rothchild, John. "The Electronic Battlefield: Wiring Down
the War." *The Washington Monthly,* May, 1971.
DMS Market Intelligence Report. (Various sections from various volumes,
1969–74.) Old Greenich, Connecticut: McGraw-Hill Inc.
Drumheller, Warren D. and Ferguson, C.A. "A Model Perimeter Detection
System—Federal Youth Center, Ashland, Kentucky." Undated paper pub-
lished by the Westinghouse Electric Corp., Pittsburgh, Pennsylvania.
Electronics. "Army Seeks First-Round Targeting Capability." December 26,
1974.
——— "Night Recon Gets a Lift from a Large-Diameter Image Intensifier."
September 5, 1974.
Elson, Benjamin M. "Laser Link Uses Stabilized Binoculars." *Aviation Week and
Space Technology,* June 29, 1970.
——— "Laser Studied as Nuclear Power Trigger." *Aviation Week and Space
Technology,* March 25, 1974.
Evans, Rowland and Novak, Robert. "Electronic Barrier." *Washington Post,*
October 8, 1967.
——— "Opposition to the War." *Washington Post,* October 8, 1967.
Famiglietti, Gene. "Can De Fence Be Ignored?" *Navy Times,* October 11, 1967.
Farrar, Fred. "Sensors Help Yanks Find Viet Enemy." *Chicago Tribune,*
February 19, 1971.
Feld, B.T., Greenwood, T., Rathjens, G.W. and Weinberg, S. *Impact of
New Technologies on the Arms Race.* Cambridge, Massachusetts: MIT Press,
1971.
Finney, John W. "Anonymous Call Set Off Rumors About Nuclear Arms for
Vietnam." *New York Times,* February 13, 1968.
——— "GAO Challenges $111-million Plane—Report Aids Critics of Air Force
System." *New York Times,* February 23, 1975.
——— "Guided Bombs Expected to Revolutionize Warfare." *New York Times,*
March 18, 1974.

———— "Pentagon Pushes for a Radar Place Capable of Directing Air Battles." *New York Times*, January 7, 1975.

———— "Pentagon to Urge Air Radar System—Schlesinger Wants Congress to Provide $4 Billion for Boeing Planes." *New York Times*, February 13, 1975.

Forsythe, Lt. Gen. George I. "The Battlefield of the Future." *Defense Industry Bulletin*, March, 1970.

Fouquet, David. "NATO Studies Costly US Radar Plane." *Washington Post*, April 25, 1975.

Fried, Joseph. "US Bugs Nip Reds in Laos." *New York Daily News*, March 19, 1968.

Frisbee, John L. "Igloo White." *Air Force*, June, 1971.

Garber, Vitalij. "Remotely Piloted Vehicles for the Army." *Astronautics and Aeronautics*, October, 1974.

Getlein, Frank. "Computers are Dangerous General." *Washington Star*, October 29, 1969.

Getler, Michael. "Generals Say Electronic Battlefield Saves Lives." *Washington Post*, November 19, 1970.

Gillette, Robert. "It Took a While to Sell the Smart Bomb." *The Sunday Star*, June 18, 1972.

Government Marketing Service. "Remotely Piloted Vehicles." Covina, California, Procurement Associates Inc., September, 1974.

Graham, William B. "RMVs in Aerial Warfare." *Astronautics and Aeronautics*, May, 1972.

Green, Larry. "US Cuts Back Sensors on Red Trail." *Washington Star-News*, December 13, 1972.

Greene, Terrell E. "Remotely Manned Systems—Origins and Current Capabilities." Paper-4809. Santa Monica, California, The RAND Corporation, February, 1972.

Gudgel, Brig. Gen. Edward F., Jr. "A Look at the Integrated Battlefield Control System (ICBS)." Undated paper distributed by the information office, Fort Belvoir, Virginia.

Hackworth, Col. David H. "Our Great Vietnam Goof!" *Popular Mechanics*, June, 1972.

Halacy, Daniel S., Jr. *Bionics, the Science of 'Living' Machines.* New York: Holiday House, 1965.

Hartt, Julian. "McNamara's Viet Wall Being Built in Arizona." *Los Angeles Times*, October 15, 1967.

Harvey, Frank. "Air War Vietnam—1972." *Worldview*, March, 1972.

Hawkes, Nigel. "Catalogue of Carnage." *World*, December 5, 1972.

Hay, Lt. Gen. John H., Jr. *Tactical and Materiel Innovations* (Vietnam Studies Series). Washington, D.C., the Department of the Army, 1974. (GPO Stock Number 0820-00471.)

Heebner, David R. "An Emerging Technology with Modest Investments." *Commander's Digest*, January 16, 1975.

Heiman, Grover. "Beep to Bang." *Armed Forces Management*, July, 1970.

Hessman, James D. "RPVs for the Navy: Unmanned Aircraft and Ships Could Revolutionize Naval Warfare." *Seapower*, August, 1973.

―――― "The Army's Big Eight: Top Priority Programs for the Seventies." *Armed Forces Journal*, November 16, 1970.

Hill, Maynard L. "Electrostatic Autopilots for Stabilization of Remotely Piloted Vehicles." 1972 Paper Available from the Applied Physics Laboratory, Johns Hopkins University, Silver Spring, Maryland.

Hilton, Col. Richard D. "What Every Ground Commander Should Know About Guided Bombs." *Army*, June, 1973.

Hughes, Clem. "These are the MASSTER Years." *US Army Aviation Digest*, August, 1974.

International Committee of the Red Cross. *Report on the Work of the Conference on the Use of Certain Conventional Weapons.* Lucerne, October 18, 1974.

―――― *Weapons that may Cause Unnecessary Suffering or Have Indiscriminate Effects.* Geneva, 1973.

Jacobson, Lt. Col. R.H. "Low Cost Tactical RPVs." Paper-4902. Santa Monica, California, the RAND Corp., September, 1972.

Keatley, Robert. "Life Along the Ho Chi Minh Trail." *Wall Street Journal*, December 1, 1971.

Keller, Eugenia. "The Electronic Battlefield." *Chemistry*, September, 1972.

Kelly, Orr. "Automated Battlefield." *Washington Star*, May 17, 1970.

―――― "Drawing a Billion Dollar Line in Vietnam." *The Virginian Pilot*, July 21, 1968.

―――― "$8 Billion a Year Spent on Technology." *Washington Star*, January 8, 1969.

―――― "Ho Trail Supply Flow Reported at a Trickle." *The Sunday Star*, January 24, 1971.

―――― "Major Test Set for Battlefield Sensor System." *The Sunday Star*, January 23, 1972.

―――― "McNamara Line—Real But Still Secret." *The Sunday Star*, July 14, 1968.

―――― "Sensors May Revolutionize Combat." *Washington Star*, June 10, 1969.

―――― "Statisticians on Ho Chi Minh Trail." *Washington Star*, August 20, 1968.

―――― "US 'Bugs' Aim Bombs at Ho Trail." *Washington Star*, January 18, 1971.

―――― "Was Vietnam War 'Won' in August?" *Washington Star*, December 17, 1968.

Kirk, Donald. "Not-So-Secret Air Raids Are Not Stopping the Enemy." *Philadelphia Inquirer*, January 28, 1972.

Klare, Michael. "The Army of the 1970s." *Nation*, January 26, 1974.

―――― *War Without End.* New York: Alfred A. Knopf, 1972.

Klass, Philip J. "A-7E, A-6 to Get Infrared Sensor." *Aviation Week and Space Technology*, April 17, 1972.

―――― "AWACS Meet Heavy Traffic Challenges." *Aviation Week and Space Technology*, May 5, 1975.

—— "Electronic Warfare Unit Expands Efforts." *Aviation Week and Space Technology*, August 5, 1974.

—— "More Laser Weapon Funds Sought." *Aviation Week and Space Technology*, May 14, 1973.

Kocivar, Ben. "The Deadly Game of Electronic Warfare." *Popular Science*, October, 1971.

Kraft, Joseph. "Policy of Creeping Gavinism Affects US Vietnam Posture." *Washington Post*, September 7, 1967.

Kresa, Kent and Kirlin, Col. William F. "The Mini-RPV, Big Potential . . . Small Cost." *Astronautics and Aeronautics*, September, 1974.

Law Enforcement Assistance Administration. *Fiscal Year 75 Project Plans: Law Enforcement Standards Laboratory* (NBSIR 74-568), Washington, D.C., September, 1974.

Lelyveld, Joseph. "Electronic Line Opposed by Laos." *New York Times*, January 25, 1968.

Lescaze, Lee. "Viet Barrier Project Pushed." *Washington Post*, April 16, 1967.

Los Angeles Times. "US Cutback Reported in Laos Trail Sensors." December 14, 1972.

Lucas, Jim G. "Mine Barrier Ordered." *Washington Daily News*, October 10, 1966.

—— " 'McNamara Line' May Go." *Washington Daily News*, November 8, 1968.

—— "When a Fence is Not a Fence." *Washington Daily News*, September 18, 1967.

Malloy, Michael. "The Death Harvesters." *Far Eastern Economic Review*, January 29, 1972.

Marine Corps Development and Education Command, *Concept for the Employment of Sensors.* DB-4-71, Quantico, Virginia, 1971.

—— *Sensors in Tactical Surveillance.* DB-5-71, Quantico, Virginia, 1971.

Mentor, John L. and Smircich, Ronald J. "Automation and Mobility." *Military Review*, November, 1970.

Messex, Maj. Curtis L. "Night on the Trail." *Air Force*, January, 1972.

Metz, William D. "Laser Fusion Secrecy Lifted: Microballoons Are the Trick." *Science*, November 8, 1974.

Middleton, Drew. "Battlefield Computers and Detection Devices Join the Army." *New York Times*, October 27, 1970.

—— "Futuristic Weapons Tested at Reservation on the Coast." *New York Times*, April 25, 1971.

—— "Spending Mounts for Laser Arms." *New York Times*, September 13, 1973.

Miller, Barry. "Cost Reductions Key to Wider FLIR Use." *Aviation Week and Space Technology*, May 21, 1973.

—— "FLIR Gaining Wider Service Acceptance." *Aviation Week and Space Technology*, May 7, 1973.

Miller, Edward A., Jr. "Controlling Inhumane Weapons." *Arms Control Today*, November, 1974.
Miller, Mike. "Even the Trees Have Ears . . ." *Washington Daily News*, September 24, 1971.
———— "Snooping Down the Ho Chi Minh Trail." *Washington Daily News*, February 18, 1971.
Mitgang, Herbert. "Sensors Don't Bleed." *New York Times*, December 20, 1971.
MITRE Corp. "Developing Sensor Systems for Defense." *MITRE Matrix* (the company's house organ), October, 1972.
Modern Army Selected Systems and Review (MASSTER). *Guide for the Employment of Unattended Ground Sensors*. Fort Hood, Texas, December, 1970.
———— *IBCS: Staff Organization and Procedures Report*. Fort Hood, Texas, September, 1972.
———— *MASSTER III Systems Field Test Scenario*. Fort Hood, Texas, March, 1973.
———— *TARS-75 Exercise Gallant Hand Evaluation Report*. Fort Hood, Texas, July, 1972.
Mohr, Charles. "Plan to Seal off Zone Considered." *New York Times*, October 12, 1966.
McLucas, John L. "The Role of the RPVs in the Air Force." *Commander's Digest*. January 16, 1975.
National Academy of Engineering. *Communications Technology for Urban Improvement*. Washington, D.C., June, 1971.
National Action/Research on the Military Industrial Complex (NARMIC.) *Automated Air War Script* (Accompanies Slide Presentation). Philadelphia, Pennsylvania, 1972.
———— *Background Report on the Automated Battlefield*. Philadelphia, Pennsylvania, 1972.
Nation's Business. "How Illegal Aliens Rob Jobs From Unemployed Americans." May, 1975.
Navy Times. "35-Pound Radar Set Detects Night Foe." January 31, 1968.
Nellor, R.A., *How to Get It—A Guide to Defense-Related Documents*. Arlington, Virginia, the Institute for Defense Analyses, October, 1973.
New York Regional Anti-War Faculty and Student Group. "Hasten JASON— Guard the Nation." *Science for the People* Magazine, September, 1972.
Newsweek. "An Electronic Picket Line at the DMZ." April 17, 1967.
———— "Drone Patrol." October 8, 1973.
———— "End of the McNamara Line." June 16, 1969.
———— "Laos: Where the Bombing Goes On." March 31, 1969.
———— "New Tools for Cops." October 7, 1974.
———— "Spotting the Infiltrators." May 27, 1968.
———— "Visions of the Next War." April 22, 1974.

Nihart, Brooke. "Army Triple Threat Division Test at Fort Hood." *Armed Forces Journal*, May 3, 1971.

O'Brien, Daniel J. and Schweizer, Paul H. "Future High Altitude RPV Applications—Impact on Design." Seattle, Washington, The Boeing Co., November 1, 1973.

Olsen, Jack. *Aphrodite: Desperate Mission.* New York: Putnam, 1970.

Ott, John J. *Scatterable Antipersonnel Mine Test Data Summary.* Fort Hood, Texas, Project MASSTER, February, 1974.

Palmer, Lt. Col. John A. "Air Force Concepts for RPV Applications." *Astronautics and Aeronautics*, October, 1974.

Parade. "FBI's Air Force." March 30, 1975.

Powers, Lt. Col. Davies R. and Newman, Richard G. "What's Next Over the Hill?" *Commander's Digest*, January 16, 1975.

Price, William. "Navy's 'Super-Snooper' Spies on Enemies in Indochina." *Philadelphia Inquirer*, March 4, 1971.

Prokosch, Eric. *The Simple Art of Murder: Antipersonnel Weapons and Their Developers.* Philadelphia, NARMIC, 1972.

Ramirez, Raul. "Washable Bullet-Proof Vest Comes in Light Blue for $99." *Washington Post*, October 3, 1972.

RAND Corporation. *Annual Report 1973–4.* Santa Monica, California.

Remotely Monitored Battlefield Sensor System (REMBASS) Project Office. *Southeast Asia Operational Sensor System (SEAOPSS) Equipment List.* Fort Monmouth, New Jersey, October, 1973, revised September 1, 1974.

Reuters. "Tiny Sensors Guided Bombers at Khesanh." *Washington Post*, April 15, 1968.

Ripley, Anthony. "Day After the 'Alert': NORAD Tells Visitors of Electronic Marvels." *New York Times*, February 22, 1971.

Roberts, Chalmers. "Vietnam Barrier Could Become Route to Conference on Peace." *Washington Post*, September 9, 1967.

Roberts, Gene. " 'People Sniffer' Follows Scent of Enemy from Copter in Delta." *New York Times*, August 18, 1968.

—— "Work on 'McNamara Line' in Vietnam Near Standstill." *New York Times*, March 25, 1968.

Robertson, Jack. "McNamara Wall Wins a Vote." *Electronic News*, May 12, 1969.

—— "US Building Intrusion Net Across Korea." *Electronic News*, August 5, 1968.

—— "Viet 'Wall' Will Sense Enemy, Flash Warning to Main HQ." *Electronic News*, October 30, 1967.

San Francisco Chronicle. "A New McNamara Line." October 26, 1970.

Schell, Orville. "Better Killing Through Electronics." *Earth*, April, 1972.

—— "The Subculture Spawned by Electronic Warfare." *Harper's*, October, 1972.

Schwartz, Charles. *Professors in the Pentagon/ JASON II.* Berkeley, Scientists and Engineers for Social and Political Action (SESPA), February, 1974.

SESPA. *Science Against the People.* Berkeley, December, 1972.

———— *The AMRC Papers.* Madison, 1973.

Seamans, Robert C. "Improving Air Force Operating Efficiency." *Air Force*, May, 1973.

Seeman, G.R., Harris, G.L., Brown, G.J., and Cullian, C.A. "Remotely Piloted Mini-Blimps for Urban Applications." *Aeronautics and Astronautics*, February, 1974.

Sell, Ted. "McNamara Wall: Sudden Death." *Los Angeles Times*, June 1, 1969.

———— "Old Indian Fort Used as Secret Test Center." *Los Angeles Times*, September 8, 1968.

Senator Gravel Edition: The Pentagon Papers. Volume IV. Boston: Beacon Press, 1971.

Shearer, Derek. "Automated War." *The New Republic.* May 30, 1970.

Siegel, Lenny. "Supercomputer." Unpublished paper from the Pacific Studies Center, East Palo Alto, California, August, 1972.

————"Vietnam's Electronic Battlefield." *Pacific Research and World Empire Telegram*, September-October, 1971.

Smith, D.A. "Educated Missiles." *Ordnance*, March-April, 1972.

Smith, Brig. Gen. Lynn D. "Facts Not Opinions." *Army*, December, 1969.

Soldiers. "Silence is Noisy." May, 1972.

Stambler, Irwin. "A Review of the American RPV Scene." *Interavia*, October, 1973.

———— "US Remotely Piloted Vehicle Programs." *International Defense Review*, February, 1974.

Stanford, Phil. "The Automated Battlefield." *The New York Times Magazine*, February 23, 1975.

Stockholm International Peace Research Institute (SIPRI). *World Armaments and Disarmaments: SIPRI Yearbook 1974.* Cambridge: The MIT Press and Stockholm, Almquist & Wiksell, 1974.

Storm, Allen. "Night Eyes on the B-52." *Air Force*, October, 1974.

Sullivan, Walter. "Rumors on Use of Atomic Arms Stirred by Experts' Asian Trips." *New York Times*, February 12, 1968.

Teledyne Ryan Aeronautical Reporter. Special issue, "Age of the RPV." Summer, 1971.

Time. "Alarm Belt." September 15, 1967.

———— "On the Horizon." September 22, 1967.

———— "The Electronic Arsenal." March 3, 1975.

———— "The Firebee." November 27, 1964.

Ulsamer, Edgar. "A-10 Approach to Close Air Support." *Air Force*, May, 1973.

———— " 'Flyable' Smart Bomb—Adding Another Dimension to Airpower." *Air Force*, August, 1972.

———— "New Muscles for the Tactical Arm." *Air Force*, October, 1974.

———— "Remotely Piloted Aircraft—Weapons Systems of the Future?" *Air Force*, October, 1970.

———— "Status Report on Laser Weapons." *Air Force*, January, 1972.

———— "USAF's R&D Riddle: How to Do More With Less?" *Air Force*, November, 1974.

United Press International. "Buoy Malfunctions Signal Enemy Attack." *Washington Post*, January 16, 1974.

———— "Sensors Credited With Saving of GIs." *Washington Post*, March 1, 1971.

US Army Munitions Command. *Laboratory Posture Report: Fiscal Year 1973*. Dover, N.J., 1974.

US Congress, House of Representatives. *Hearings on Military Posture and Department of Defense Authorization for Appropriations for Fiscal Year 1975*. Committee on Armed Services, Washington, D.C., 1974.

US Congress, Senate. *Hearings of the Electronic Battlefield Subcommittee of the Preparedness Investigating Subcommittee: Investigation Into Electronic Battlefield Program*. Committee on Armed Services, Washington, D.C. 1970. And the final committee report issued March 1, 1971.

———— *Hearings on the Fiscal 1975 Authorization for Military Procurement, Research and Development, and Active Duty, Selected Reserve, and Civilian Personnel Strengths*. Committee on Armed Services, Washington, D.C., 1974.

———— *Hearings on the Fiscal Year 1976 and July–September 1976 Transition Period Authorization for Military Procurement, Research and Development, and Active Duty, Selected Reserve, and Civilian Personnel Strengths*. Committee on Armed Services, Washington, D.C., 1975.

———— *Laos: April, 1971*. Committee Print of the Committee on Foreign Relations, Washington, D.C., August 3, 1971.

US News and World Report. "Close Up of McNamara's Fence—How it Works, Why It's Disputed." January 1, 1968.

———— "McNamara's Line: It's Still Abuilding, But . . ." March 25, 1968.

University of Kentucky College of Engineering. *Carnahan Conference on Electronic Crime Countermeasures Proceedings*. 1968–1974. Lexington, Kentucky.

Verble, Keith E. and Malven, Charles J. "Precision Laser Target Designation—A Breakthrough in Guided Weapons Employment." *International Defense Review*, Number 2, 1974.

Washington Daily News. "US is Flying Pilotless Planes Over North Vietnam." November 18, 1964.

Washington Evening Star. "850 Peer at Sensors, the Warfare of Future." January 7, 1970.

Washington Post. "Goldwater Hints US Combat in Laos." July 15, 1970.

———— "The Barrier" (editorial). September 9, 1967.

Weaver, Kenneth. "Remote Sensing: New Eyes to See the World." *National Geographic*, January, 1969.

Weiss, George. "CO 2/17 AIR CAV: 'Gunships to Tanks, Survived Flak' in Laos." *Armed Forces Journal*, April 19, 1971.

――― "SEA Sensor Fields: More Eyes and Ears." *Armed Forces Journal*, March 1, 1971.

――― "The Air Force's Secret Electronic War." *Military Aircraft*, 1971.

Westing, Arthur H. "The Super Bomb." *American Report*, September 8, 1972.

Westmoreland, Gen. W.C. Address at the annual luncheon of the Association of the US Army, Washington, D.C., October 14, 1969.

――― "The Army in Transition." *Ordnance*, July-August 1971.

Wilson, Andrew. *The Bomb and the Computer.* New York: The Delacorte Press, 1968.

Wilson, George C. "Hill to Probe Sensor Plans of Pentagon." *Washington Post*, August 20, 1970.

――― "Official Hails Detectors Along Ho Chi Minh Trail." *Washington Post*, May 1, 1969.

――― "Pentagon Studies Effectiveness of Electronic Barrier in Vietnam." *Washington Post*, October 17, 1968.

――― "US Builds Barricade Inside Laos." *Washington Post*, January 1, 1968.

――― "Viet-Barrier Plans Restudied by US." *Washington Post*, January 15, 1967.

Woodbridge, C.L. *Unattended Ground Sensors.* Washington, D.C., the MITRE Corp., March, 1963.

Wyant, E. "Computer Security Management at Walt Disney World." Paper from RCA Corporate Engineering Services, March 1, 1973.

INDEX

THE ELECTRONIC BATTLEFIELD

BY PAUL DICKSON

Automatic weapons systems that not only fire themselves but *make the decision* when to fire—a new breed of unmanned aircraft capable of shooting down the fastest manned fighter planes now in the air—a low-flying missile able to read maps—remote sensing devices capable of monitoring the coming and going of others over vast distances—new, laser-guided weapons that alone revolutionize the business of killing—these are only a few of the highly sophisticated features of the battlefield of the 1980s. Extraordinary changes in military technology—with broad logistic, tactical, and moral implications—are now under way at a cost of billions of dollars and without benefit of public debate or consideration. The concept of an electronic or automated battlefield is little understood outside military circles; this book clearly sets forth the astonishing facts about it for a wider audience.

The Electronic Battlefield begins by examining the novel, prophetic, and often horrific handiwork of the ultrasecret group, code-named Jasons, who developed the new sensing devices and related technology which have done for conventional warfare what the nuclear/missile revolution did for all-out war. Dickson shows how the one